When the seeking's over,
the joy begins.

RECOVERY PLUS
Freedom From
Co-dependency

Joe Alexander
with Rowena Alexander

Health Communications, Inc.
Deerfield Beach, Florida

© 1991 Joe Alexander
ISBN 1-55874-106-2

Publisher: Health Communications, Inc.
3201 S.W. 15th Street
Deerfield Beach, Florida 33442-8190

Cover design by Graphic Expressions

Dedication

This book is for all those people in recovery who keep on keeping on in the struggle to find meaning, purpose and fulfillment in their lives.

Author's Note

This book is about real people. To protect their anonymity their names and the circumstances under which I encountered them have been altered. Where surnames have been used, permission to do so has been granted by the persons named.

Acknowledgments

My first appreciation is always for my wife, Rowena, who has been my friend, lover, confidant and companion for more than 50 years.

I am forever grateful to Bob and Mary Goulding for pointing out to me that autonomy is an option and I could choose to redecide my life directions in favor of authenticity and autonomy. Their pioneering work in redecision therapy inspired me to get on with living life my way, teaching and writing about the "how to's" of autonomy and self-actualization.

Many thanks go to Ed Frost, psychotherapist and friend, who once again has "listened" me through a book's long gestation and delivery. With Ed I have a special kind of autonomous friendship not known to many men.

I am grateful to Marie Stilkind of Health Communications for having asked me the right question at the right time. Looking at my own adult child issues and co-dependency gave me a whole new field of exploration and challenge at a time of life when I might have been sitting on the sidelines, feeling sorry for myself because I'd let life pass me by.

Though I've never met or seen Gail Sheehy, I have a special regard for her research and writing. In *Passages* and *Pathfinders* I found many helpful guidelines for making the journey that lies beyond middle age.

After attending a class taught by Janet Hurley concerning relationships in recovery, I realized the practical value of transactional analysis as a working tool for recovery from co-dependency. I especially thank her for the many strategies and exercises I've learned from her and adapted for my own teaching.

I am also thankful to the new breed of professionals in the behavioral sciences who have based their writings on their own experiences rather than on the wanderings of some rat in a maze. There are many of them but the writers who have been most helpful to me are Melody Beattie, John Bradshaw, Pia Mellody and Janet Woititz.

In the course of getting this book in its present shape, Hal Bennett has been a patient mentor, editor and agent, one who works as much from his heart as from his mind. He protects me from the people-pleaser in me and gently reminds me that I am not the Hemingway I once dreamed of being.

My thanks also to the hundreds of people in workshops, classes and self-help groups who have helped me so much while helping themselves.

Table Of Contents

Introduction

I never suspected that I would have to learn how to live — that there were specific disciplines and ways of seeing the world I had to master before I could awaken to a simple, happy, uncomplicated life.

— Dan Millman

Except for improved health and a salvaged marriage, four years of abstinence from alcohol didn't bring me the serenity and successful living I had expected. Instead it brought me face to face with a midlife crisis and the helpless, hopeless feelings that come when no light can be seen at the end of the tunnel. Some call this condition a long-term "dry drunk" or "the second bottom."

My recovery from the "dis-ease" that touches many of us in abstinence began when I struck out in the direction of autonomy, seeking freedom from attitudes and actions that had worked for me in younger days but were failing me in my 40s. Even though I didn't know where I was coming from, I began moving away from what is now known as co-dependency. I began moving toward the freedom to be myself, doing what I chose to do in the world, rather than continuing on a path laid down for me by others who had themselves never mastered the art of successful living. Without a map to guide me, I embarked on a journey that has been for 20 years a challenging, creative, productive and joyful way of living.

One team of investigators studying a group of sober alcoholics reported 54 percent as overtly disturbed, 24 percent as living life inadequately, 12 percent as "AA successes" with their social life and identity centered around Alcoholics Anonymous, and 10 percent considered to be achieving a state of self-respecting independence or self-realization. (1)

Had I taken that test, I would probably have been included among the 24 percent judged to be "living life inadequately." It might have been called "survival without serenity." I was frustrated and anxious: frustrated because what had always worked for me suddenly wasn't working any more and anxious because my old life script called for "crossing bridges before you come to them" and I couldn't even see any bridges. I'd run out of tomorrows at age 50 and that left me with a bunch of queasy feelings.

If you've ever been stuck with a puzzling problem and thought, "How did I get myself into this mess?" and felt stupid and worthless because you didn't know how to get out of it, you know the kind of feelings I had. I'd never heard of midlife crisis, male menopause, existential crisis, life-script crisis, or any of the other descriptions of being "stuck in time." When the past is crowding your future so tightly you don't know what the hell is going on in the present. I wanted to change but didn't know what to change from or what to change to.

If I'd known I was an adult child of an alcoholic, I wouldn't have known what to do about it. "ACoA-ism" at that time was not a subject of scientific investigation and the characteristics of ACoAs as such were yet to be reported by clinical observers. Co-dependency — a pattern of self-defeating thinking, feeling, perceiving and doing habits — was a long way away from recognition by either amateurs or professionals in the recovery field.

Even if I had known about co-dependency, I couldn't have owned up to being anything less than the "man" I'd always felt was "the only way for a male to be." Unconsciously seeking approval from the voices in my mind, I'd chosen careers that "men" did: the U.S. Border Patrol, security specialist in Venezuela and then 13 years selling in the investment and insurance business to prove myself as a man who "stood on his own two feet." Long before John Wayne popularized the term, I saw myself as living life in "True Grit" fashion.

All this time I was hiding the part of me that really wanted someone to take me by the hand and guide me through life. My survival as a boy and as a man had depended on perceiving myself as independent, so much so that I had scorned those who didn't match my vision of manhood. Machismo had shielded me from dealing with any of the feelings which went with being "less than a man."

Nevertheless, in abstinence the awareness slowly grew that problems other than alcoholism stood between me and my dreams of living life on my own terms. Abstinence brought with it many more questions than answers about my life directions.

For the first time since early adulthood, without alcohol to fuel my dreams, I was living in a world of reality. And reality offered little of the stuff my dreams were made of. What I didn't know was that my script had run out. My belief system, like obsolete programming in a computer system, was no longer appropriate to getting on with a lifelong search for being my own man.

I was stuck at a fork in the road. One way led toward self-responsibility, autonomy and self-actualization. The other led to no more than survival, living as I'd always lived, following the beat of others' drums.

Important as this discovery was in beginning my transition toward self-direction, I had no comprehension of what was going on with me. Having enjoyed a state of illusory independence for most of my drinking years, the frustration of a few non-drinking years left my mind a mess.

What had worked for me in the past just wasn't working in the present and offered meager hope for the future. People happy in their sobriety would say to me, "This too will pass." But "this" didn't pass. All that passed was time until I set out blindly in search of what it was I wanted out of life. Preoccupied as I had been for years with things like "bottom-line figures" and the Dow-Jones averages, any thoughts of autonomy, self-realization, identity, self-fulfillment or self-actualization were simply beyond my ken.

Which Way Next?

Whether you are an adult child of an alcoholic, a co-dependent, an abstinent alcoholic or — as I am — a combination of all three, you probably know how it feels to arrive at an impasse wondering, "Which way next?"

Maybe you've asked yourself sometimes, "What went wrong? How did I get here?" Maybe you've also wondered how it would be if you were someplace else, anyplace else — just so it wasn't here.

I couldn't have seen at age 51 that my search for self would lead me to a Master's degree in human communications at age 55, four years of training in group psychotherapy, and 15 years

xvi   Recovery Plus

as an independent researcher, teacher and writer in the field of successful human behavior. After I'd done all that, I thought I'd gone all the way there was to go on my path of growing up emotionally. I didn't really expect at age 70 to be making any more great discoveries about myself.

I was wrong. I don't know how I'd done all that and never once heard a word of the emerging information concerning adult children of alcoholics and co-dependency. When our daughter Lynn first began talking about adult children of alcoholics, I thought she might be trying to avoid responsibility for her own adult life problems and playing a game of "If it weren't for . . . (him, her, them or it)" with me. "If it weren't for Daddy, everything in my life would be okay."

As time went on I realized Lynn wasn't into playing blame games with me. She was into becoming her own person and was making great discoveries in her pursuit of freedom from the negative influences of her childhood programming and the co-dependency that followed in its wake.

As I listened to her wondering about the possibility of alcoholism in the family bloodline and sensed the seriousness of her effort to become an individual, living by her own standards and values instead of mine, I became an ally to her cause. I began doing what I could to help with answers to her questions about the dysfunctional dynamics of our family system.

In doing that, I didn't realize until later how much I was getting for myself in finding some answers about my own childhood development and how it had affected my adult life. Nor did I guess the added bonus that would come as I became increasingly aware of the ongoing struggle my wife, Rowena, had endured in coping with her co-dependency. Neither did I anticipate how much I would be rewarded for my efforts in getting to higher levels of tolerance and acceptance.

It was no secret that Rowena had spent her childhood locked into a family atmosphere of violence provoked by her father's alcoholism. The disease ended his life at 46 in a county hospital alone, alienated from family love.

My father had gone out of my life when I was four. Just why was a family secret never shared with me in childhood. I only have three memories of him. I do know he was Irish, a blue-collar worker and a devout but divorced Catholic who had a taste for whiskey and committed a violent suicide at age 46. From what the experts tell me, that all adds up to alcoholism.

However, my childhood programming, other than a genetic predisposition for alcoholism, was affected more by his absence than his presence.

Sharing with Lynn what I could remember of my chaotic childhood gave me good feelings about helping her in her struggles of recovery. It was almost like the years when I'd been Daddy and she'd been a little girl. It gave me a feeling of reconnection, of doing something together, some sense of walking a mutual path. It renewed a feeling lost years before when I was struggling with the efforts of "being somebody," "making a living" and seriously practicing my alcoholism.

Discovering ACoA-ism And Co-dependency

At Lynn's suggestion I read Janet Woititz's book *Adult Children of Alcoholics*. When I read her list of common characteristics of adult children of alcoholics, I knew immediately I'd found my tribe. All 13 characteristics in that list fit for me in one degree or another. My first thought was, "Now they tell me!"

I reacted to this ACoA information with puzzlement. I wondered how being the adult child of an alcoholic could be so different from what used to be called neurotic. And even though I'd long since given up my macho image, I wasn't too keen on exploring the possibility that that image had been no more than a shield protecting me from any thoughts of being something less than a *man* as I had seen *men* portrayed in the silent movies of my boyhood.

My next reaction might have been akin to those of the explorers in 1799 who discovered the Rosetta Stone that unlocked the secret for deciphering ancient Egyptian hieroglyphics. By awakening to the realities of ACoA-ism I made another wholly unexpected self-discovery. I discovered the concept of co-dependency. This sharpened my awareness and acceptance of the extent to which my dependency on others had unconsciously continued in my adult life and negatively affected my careers, my self-esteem and my relationships with others.

Perhaps if I'd made those discoveries 25 years or so ago I might have saved a whole bunch of time and money as well as a bundle of pain. As an amateur philosopher once said in a workshop, "You have to do what you have to do and what you did got you where you are today."

And doing what I did made the writing of this book possible. My hope is that it may trigger some good discoveries for you in your efforts to become an autonomous, self-actualizing person. My wish is that you will discover the freedom to be yourself as you choose to be and do what you choose to do in the pursuit of your overall well-being, the enjoyment of your life and your relationships. All of this adds up to successful living.

❧ 1 ❧

A Beginner's Steps
To Self-Understanding

Life moves on, and we, flames of the light in a prison of our own devising, must move on likewise, or be left behind.

— **Christmas Humphreys**

For more than 25 years now I've been a participant in, observer of and professional guide to small groups of people looking for better ways to increase the quality of their well-being. Four strong personal beliefs arising from that experience are:

1. *Knowing where you're coming from is sometimes more important than knowing where you want to go.* Not knowing who you are leaves knowing who you want to be more to fate than to intention. Though we all may have been born to win, most of us surrendered our autonomy to adaptations we saw as necessary to our childhood survival. Understanding that surrender and the childhood adaptation process that goes with it is a part of knowing "where you're coming from" and is essential to the recapture of the autonomy that is your birthright.

2. *Surrendering your "differentness" and accepting your linkage with others joined in a common cause is a gateway to constructive personal change.* Accepting the human need for affiliation is an antidote to the alienation that arises out of growing up in dys-

1

functional circumstances. Though recovery from ACoA-ism
and dysfunctional thinking, feeling, perceiving and doing habits
is an individual matter, knowing we are not alone gives comfort
in our travels forward.

3. *One way or another we must make every effort to break through
the barriers of denial, avoidance and projection by which we con ourselves into believing we are something we are not.* Objective analysis
of self demands that we see ourselves as we really are rather
than what we've long perceived ourselves as being. Childhood
illusions of self adopted as protection against the pain attached
to growing up in a disturbed family environment are usually
dysfunctional when continued in adulthood. As it's long been
said, "As the twig is bent, so grows the tree."

If you would straighten the childhood tree in adulthood you
first must see it as it really is and not the way you have imagined
it to be. Successful self-analysis demands objectivity, some standards for comparison and some guidelines for self-examination.

4. *Positive, creative action brings salvation from ACoA-ism and co-
dependency, a step at a time.* Every self-determined action is a step
away from co-dependency and a step toward autonomy.

Life Scripts And Co-dependency

A life script is an unconscious blueprint for living decided on
in childhood. It reflects children's reactions to the circumstances
of their family environment, how they feel about themselves
and their relationships with others, and their decisions about
how to handle themselves in the world. In *Born To Win* Muriel
James and Dorothy Jongeward define a script briefly as ". . . a
life plan, very much like a dramatic stage production, that an
individual feels compelled to act out." (1)

It is the compulsion to "act out" a life script that binds people
to a state of co-dependency for the course of their adult lives,
endlessly acting out attitudes and actions learned in childhood.
Unless these attitudes and actions are "unlearned" and replaced
by positive ones, co-dependents remain "script-bound." They
unconsciously continue their commitment to unhappy patterns
of thoughts, emotions and behaviors that echo the stresses of
early childhood development.

Life scripts can be changed. Knowing more about how you
got to be the way you are can help you change yours, freeing
you from the attitudes and actions of co-dependency. Knowing

that change is possible and understanding more about the human potential for successful living can be a needed stimulus for getting on with living life the way you want to. Knowing how others have given up their co-dependency in favor of self-dependency can reinforce your motivation to change and provide encouragement as you move in new directions. Helping you do that more effectively than I did is my motivation for writing this book.

Autonomy Or Co-dependency?

Autonomy, as the word is used here, means to be free and clear of negative thinking, feeling, perceiving and behaving habits decided on in childhood. Autonomy is diminished in direct proportion to the extent that one's life course is dictated by the illusion that individual needs are best served by serving the needs of others.

Autonomy can be numerically rated on a scale:

1 .... **10**
(Co-dependency,   (Autonomy,
** other-directed)   inner-directed)**

My childhood programming included many messages that boiled down to, "What will people think?" For years my career, clothes, marriage, parenting and leisure activities conformed to my desire to be seen favorably by "them," an imagined jury in my mind. I surrendered my identity to pleasing others.

As a child I'd not been offered a choice between co-dependency and autonomy. As an adult I'd gone along with my past programming until it became evident that the attitudes and actions of co-dependency stood between me and what I wanted out of life.

With denial slowly giving way to reality came the growing realization that in adulthood co-dependency and autonomy are choices. I could choose to stay stuck in co-dependency or I could choose to begin moving further up the autonomy scale.

And you can do the same.

Transcending People-Pleasing

Along with many other ACoAs and co-dependents I long shared a common trait of "people-pleasing." In management and sales I used this trait functionally, serving the interests of my employers and clients as well as my needs for making a living. However, as it became clear to me that "making a life" meant more to me than "making a living," my people-pleasing seemed little more than a calculated manipulation to gain my own ends. I might despise a client's political views but would "shine him on" by agreeing with him, even though I felt disgusted with myself for my lack of integrity.

When my childhood trait of people-pleasing became dysfunctional to my adult well-being, I suffered what I call an *"autonomy deficiency disorder."* My emotional disturbance reflected a clash between old childhood tapes and an increasing urge to live life on my own terms rather than those laid down for me in childhood.

I was sick and tired of hassling myself about the future and suffering the pains of body, mind and spirit that go with uncertainty, indecision and anxiety in the present. I became a middle-class dropout. I simply stopped my world and got off. One day I was wearing a grey flannel suit and wingtip brogues and the next I changed to blue jeans and sandals.

Letting go of the illusion that my happiness depended on pleasing others all the time was a beginning step in the direction of self-determination. Without knowing what I was doing, I had begun the reprogramming process that eventually would bring me to a comfortable state of autonomy, freedom to be and do as I chose.

Paradoxically, the better I served my needs for autonomy, the better I served the needs of those close to me and the world I live in. The more freely I exercised the power of choice in my interactions with others, the better I was able to meet their needs to be themselves. The more autonomy I gained, the more I was able to accept it in others. Learning to accept my wife as she is, rather than the way I want her to be, though sometimes still a struggle, is the most loving gift I can give her. And the same is true of my relationships with our adult children.

Autonomy And Appropriate Action

Appropriate action is the evidence of autonomy. What's appropriate is what's functional and effective in relationship to your goals in life. Appropriate action is keeping one eye on your chosen horizon and one eye on the path at your feet as you take the next step toward what you want. Inappropriate action is stumbling along the path you think you "should" or "ought to" follow.

Functionality can be measured on a scale:

1 10
(Nonfunctional)   **(Functional)**

Effectiveness can be measured the same way.

However, functionality and effectiveness are not necessarily synonomous. Harry, for example, is a recovering alcoholic and a public accountant who wants to be a Certified Public Accountant. He has always had a problem with procrastination, a symptom of his co-dependency, and he just doesn't get around to doing all the study required to become a Certified Public Accountant.

Harry's abstinence is highly functional in regard to his gainful employment as a public accountant. He scores a ten on being functional. However, constantly putting off the studies necessary to advance his career drops his score on effectiveness to a three. If Harry is to achieve his goal, he needs to bring his effectiveness rating up to a nine or ten. Getting professional help for his procrastination problem would be appropriate action toward his goal of becoming a CPA.

Christmas Humphreys, an English Buddhist, gave me a rule I've found fundamental to the achievement of my goals in life. In his little book, *Walk On*, he says that no matter what our goals in life, spiritual or worldly, the most important step we take in their direction is the next step. (2)

While trying to escape the pains of childhood, I learned to live in a fanciful tomorrow. As an adult, learning to live a day at a time in the present was a torturous process as I sought my escape from alcoholism and then from my white-knuckled anxiety in abstinence.

Experience has since taught me that walking on, a step at a time, is what growth of any kind is all about. It's taking risks, it's learning by experience, it's finding out what works and fixing what doesn't. Even if the next step is scary, take it anyway. When nothing's ventured, nothing's gained but regrets.

Something that has worked for me is the *Four-A-Way* for making change: *A*wareness, *A*cceptance, *A*nalysis and *A*ctualization.

The Four-A-Way Of Making Change

Awareness

The fact that you are reading this book shows you are willing to expand your awareness of the possibility that your adult life course has been negatively affected by your childhood programming. Along with that awareness you have also probably come to realize that others suffering life problems similar to yours have changed, or are changing, in search of a more satisfying life.

The greatest awareness of all is to discover you are not alone. There is solace in knowing that others have walked this path of personal growth before you and others are walking it with you now.

Acceptance

To *identify* yourself as an adult child of an alcoholic or a co-dependent is not the same as *accepting* yourself as such. To be aware that there are common traits and disorders of ACoA-ism and co-dependency is one thing. To accept those traits or disorders is another.

Covering up our perceived deficiencies in childhood was a habit. For self-protection we learned to live an imaginary life, fancying ourselves to be something other than we were. The image we created of ourselves, whether okay or not okay, was necessary to our psychological survival. Our imaginations provided sanctuary from the mind-splitting ambiguities of our daily lives. Delusion protected us from the disturbing thought that we might not be okay, either with ourselves or with the rest of the world.

Sooner or later in adulthood these delusions come into conflict with the world of reality, as childhood assumptions are tested by experience and maturity. Crisis confronts us when we begin to see the world as it really is instead of the way we thought it was going to be.

Sometimes we are unwilling to see ourselves as others see us so we close our eyes to reality. We do what we can to hang onto our illusions. We shirk responsibility for the havoc that arises in our lives. We shrink from accepting ourselves. We hesitate to confront our need for change.

In denial we refuse to recognize certain facts as they are. In avoidance we minimize the negative effect of our attitudes and actions on our well-being and that of others important to us. In projection we disassociate ourselves from our faults and attribute them to others.

To accept yourself as you are — ACoA, co-dependent or any combination thereof — is no lessening of personal worth. You are not your symptoms. You are you, the sum total of your heritage, your childhood programming and your adult experience. Whatever that all adds up to, you have the right and the capacity to change. If the quality of well-being in your life is not up to that you wish to enjoy, accept yourself as you are. You can't know how you're doing in life until you accept "where you're at" in comparison to where you want to go.

Analysis

Self-analysis is not to be engaged in as compulsively self-administered psychoanalysis. It is not to be engaged in as an obsessive preoccupation with the "whys" of your existence. Rather it is an invitation to discover the "how comes" of your life: a self-examination of your childhood programming and your belief system. It is a measurement of how functional and effective you are in the management of your life course today.

Self-analysis speaks to several questions: "How come I came to be the person I am today? How come I believe the things I do? How come I do things the way I do, especially when my actions so often sabotage my best intentions in this business of living?"

The "how comes" in life are rooted in the early decisions we made about ourselves and the adaptations we made to our environment, believing them to be necessary to our well-being. In *Games People Play* Eric Berne suggests:

1. We start out life in an autonomous state being capable of awareness, autonomy and intimacy.
2. Our parents, deliberately or otherwise, teach us how to think, feel, perceive and behave the way they think we "should" or "ought to."
3. In the interests of our early childhood survival we adapt to the family rules and surrender our potential for autonomy.

4. Because those adaptations are "in the nature of a series of decisions" they can be undone since "decisions are reversible under favorable circumstances." (3)

The task of analysis is to uncover the childhood adaptations and original decisions that committed us to putting others' needs above our own. The intensity of those commitments determines the degree of co-dependency affecting our life course in the present.

Uncovering the early childhood decisions that negatively affected my adult life course was not an overnight task. And I only made those discoveries with the help of guides skilled in exploring the archaic messages and old feeling habits embedded in my memory bank. Even with their help it took a lot of work, a lot of pain and a surrender of my over-reliance on logic to accept the fact that I had been running my life according to a plan decided on by an eight-year-old boy.

Eventually I awakened to the fact that those early childhood decisions could be "redecided," that I could rewrite my co-dependent script and that the quality of my well-being was my responsibility. Recognizing that the thinking, feeling, perceiving and doing habits of a co-dependent were only habits, helped me develop a new life plan, a self-directed one for positive, creative living.

You can do that, too. You can give up your blind adherence to childhood family rules and the attitudes and actions of co-dependency. You can develop a positive belief system and functional, effective behavioral habits once you've learned to "track down" the co-dependency messages in your mind, "redecide" the negative in favor of the positive, and get on with the action necessary to achieve autonomy. Patience and persistence will lead to the positive payoffs that come with being self-dependent.

Actualization

Actualization is getting on with doing the things that need to be done for you to become all that you choose to be in life. Autonomy and actualization are the essence of successful living.

With some awareness of the need to escape from co-dependency, a healthy acceptance of yourself as you are, some analysis of your habits and at least a rough plan of action, your next step is to find a method for making constructive changes in your life. Finding that method and deciding how you will go about learning it is a major task.

Once you have established a sound operating method to resolve conflict between your inner and outer worlds, the way will be open to whatever level of self-dependence and self-fulfillment is necessary to your life satisfaction. Once you've made that system work for you, you can go on using it successfully for as long as you choose to stay on the path of growth.

At least that's the way it's gone for me since I made the great discovery that full recovery means more than just recovery from alcoholism. It also means recovery from *me*. It means recovery from co-dependency and the after-effects of growing up in my dysfunctional family system, the kind Robert Subby describes in his book *Lost In The Shuffle* as the Emotionally Disturbed and Rigid Dogmatic family. (4)

For years I'd thought about recovery as a one-track process: You get dry, clean, or otherwise free from addiction and get on with getting what you want out of life.

Now I see recovery as a two-track process with abstinence running on one track and recovery from co-dependency running on the other. Both are lifetime tracks and both are mandatory to the achievement of full recovery, something I choose to call successful living.

The redecision process I learned from Bob and Mary Goulding and the reprogramming method I developed on my own brought me up most days from about a four on the life satisfaction scale to about a nine. And that's not bad for a guy who once seemed destined for the fate of Willy Lohman in *Death Of A Salesman*.

What others have done you can do. You can upgrade the quality of your well-being in a similar fashion if you choose to, decide to and are willing to get on with resolving the co-dependency issues that have kept you from the fullest enjoyment of a creative, productive and meaningful life.

On the journey ahead take comfort from these words of Ruth Fishel: "Stay with it, be with it, go through it and learn from it, no matter what." Ruth, in recovery from alcoholism and ACoA-ism, also wrote in *The Journey Within*, "Hiding is no longer an option if you want to live." (5)

Co-dependency is a closet and the knob on the door works from the inside as well as the outside. I didn't get out of my closet till I was willing to open the door from the inside and take my chances in the world of reality. As you've probably already learned, some pain is unavoidable on the path of change; but remind yourself that still being in the race proves you are a survivor.

Why not take the next step forward and get on with becoming self-dependent and a happy survivor?

❦ 2 ❦

How We Surrendered Ourselves To Others' Expectations

Each human being is born as something new, something that never existed before. He is born with what he needs to win at life. Each person in his own way can see, hear, touch, taste and think for himself. Each has his own unique potentials — his capabilities and limitations. Each can be a significant, thinking, aware, and creatively productive person in his own right — a winner.

— **Muriel James and Dorothy Jongeward**

You were born with a potential to achieve autonomy and self-actualization.

Autonomous people march to the beat of their own drums. They live by current choice, free of compulsive commitment to attitudes and actions decided on for childhood survival. They are comfortably detached from the myth that all self-satisfaction depends on satisfying the needs of others. They take full responsibility for the quality of their well-being as self-dependent rather than co-dependent adults.

Self-actualizing people do what they need to do to satisfy their deep inner needs to live creative, productive and meaningful lives. They are successful from the inside out rather than the outside in.

11

Autonomous and self-actualizing people are comfortable with themselves and comfortable to live and work with. They are content to live the lives they've chosen and be with those they choose as life companions. They feel good about themselves and their choices. They are clear about their identity, are open to learning by experience and enjoy high levels of self-regard.

That's some list of qualities for mere mortals. And if it's good and desirable to be an autonomous, self-actualizing human being, why aren't more of us like that?

Because, like an estimated 96 percent of the population, we suffer from co-dependency to one degree or another. We cling to habits of thinking, feeling, perceiving and doing what we learned a long time ago for physical, emotional and spiritual survival. We surrendered our individual wants, needs and expectations in favor of the needs, wants, expectations and demands of others.

We did that because in many cases, maybe most, those "others" were representatives of a dysfunctional family system. Raised in an environment inhabited by physical or emotional illness, alcoholism, drug addiction, authoritarianism or religion addiction, we did what we could to get by. We adapted and survived our childhood, though not without wounds we have yet to heal.

In adulthood the trick is to move on from being a survivor to becoming a Winner — an autonomous, self-actualizing person. For some this process of personal growth just happens. They move easily through life as they learn from experience. Little is known about these natural winners, but it seems fair to assume they were blessed with birth into a loving, accepting, fully functional family.

Childhood Decisions And Life Directions

Unfortunately, few of us move through life like that. The potential for autonomy that came with birth gets stomped on in varying degrees by parents, teachers, peers and others. Consciously or unconsciously, our own lack of autonomy and our bondage to co-dependency rules our behaviors in ways crippling to healthy childhood development. As Scott Peck, author of *The Road Less Traveled*, says, "Everybody comes from a dysfunctional family. The only question is 'How dysfunctional?'" (1)

Each of us in our own way adapted to the circumstances of our familial, cultural and social environment. We were pushed toward conformity and surrender of our wants to the "shoulds" and "ought tos" of those we sought to please in the hopes that our efforts would bring us the love we needed and wanted. Rightly or wrongly we decided whether we were OK, whether others were OK and what attitudes and actions would make us OK with others. Dependent on the approval of others, we learned by experience to put aside our needs and serve their needs.

Because we lacked information, skills and support for being ourselves, our decisions were purely survival responses; the attitudes and actions perceived necessary to our needs for physical and emotional well-being. In direct proportion to the rewards and recognition or putdowns and punishments we received for our performance, we decided how we felt about ourselves and how we stood in the eyes of others.

We decided on the adaptations of mind and body we perceived necessary to our survival in our environment. We decided what roles we'd play, the way we'd play them and — with no awareness on our part of doing so — we ordained the course our lives would follow.

Most of these early childhood decisions might well be described as "happenings," an evolutionary course of attitude and action that unconsciously made sense in childhood. When the family rule is "Silence is golden" (Don't talk), we learn to avoid the negative strokes that go with "speaking up." We give up our right to question, challenge or demonstrate any other spontaneous expression of autonomy. If that rule is harshly enforced, physically or emotionally, it is doubly powerful.

My wife, Rowena, once asked her alcoholic father if she could spend the night with a girl friend and was refused. When she asked "Why?" he slapped her in the face and said, "Because I said so, that's why." Though that was the only time he ever physically abused her, it was symbolic of a family rule that dictated, "Don't talk back to your superiors." That slap reinforced a "Don't talk" message in Rowena's human software. Except when very pressured, it is extremely difficult for her to be assertive. The intensity of that message was further strengthened by her mother's saying many times, "You just can't talk to a man."

Eventually Rowena came to believe that message. Without ever consciously deciding to do so, she programmed into her belief system a strong message, "Men never listen." Regretfully my years of drinking did little to help her overcome her nonassertiveness or her distrust of men in general.

Some children make conscious decisions about what goes on with them and what to do about it. In a counseling session, Jake told of many beatings by his father. He said, "I told them all (family) I'd run away when I was ten and never come back."

I said, "What did they say?"

"They laughed at me. But I showed 'em. I ain't never been back."

"Think you might ever make peace with your father?"

"No way." The tightening of his jaws signaled the end of that discussion.

His anger and determination to "show them" was a coping mechanism that had permitted his survival in a dysfunctional family. In adulthood "showing them" had driven him to some small successes as a building contractor, but the anger fueling that drive played havoc with his man-woman relationships.

In adulthood both Rowena and Jake, like so many others, were co-dependent with the child within, the childlike part of our personality that continues to exert its influences over us, even though we are chronologically grown up. (This is detailed in *Healing The Child Within* by Charles Whitfield.) They continued to follow the life scripts they'd decided on in childhood. In time, Rowena chose to moderate her co-dependency and opened herself to increased intimacy in our relationship. Jake chose to stay stuck in his Rock-of-Gibraltar role. His marriage went down the drain and as far as I know, he's still "running away from home."

Rowena wished that somehow life would change and be better. Jake didn't. Her hope was faint but she believed, even though she didn't know how such change could come about. She still clung to her deeply-embedded message, "Life's a struggle." Every night she prayed, and still does:

> *Now I lay me down to sleep*
> *I pray the Lord my soul to keep*
> *If I should die before I wake*
> *I pray the Lord my soul to take.*

That prayer, however, only promotes her faith in the hereafter. Having faith to be in charge of herself in the here and now has always been difficult for her.

If you have doubts about your future and question your capacity for recovery from co-dependency, consider the words of

Dr. Timmen L. Cermak (who describes himself as a congenital co-dependent): "The only avenue toward recovery requires a leap of faith long before anyone feels ready for it." (2) Each step taken, each lesson learned on the path of personal change will add to your faith in yourself and your capabilities for moving on toward self-dependency.

Co-dependent Scripts

There were many times as I struggled along in the early years of my anxiety-plagued abstinence that I wondered if some unknown force had destined me to endless repetitions of the past. I'd impulsively embark on some new endeavor, sail along euphorically for a year or two then find fault with what I was doing. As the fire of my enthusiasm burned down, I'd suffer a "personality clash" with my superior or "come to realize" my employers were really heartless rascals who cared little about those of us who served them and even less for the public they served. I'd leave, compelled by a grandiose image of myself as a "man of honor," only to go do the same thing all over again.

Looking back I could identify a definite pattern that dogged me in my efforts to "become somebody." I was beginning to realize that history does repeat itself in the lives of persons as well as nations. This was soon confirmed in my earliest encounters with the life-script theories of Eric Berne. He wrote, "A script is an ongoing program, developed in early childhood under parental influence, which directs the individual's behavior in the most important aspects of his life." (3)

Almost 20 years later I learned about co-dependency and realized it is what life scripts are all about, a self-inflicted wounding of one's well-being. A co-dependent life script may dictate all or any of the following: low self-esteem, compulsive behavior such as inappropriate caretaking or rescuing of others, anxiety when either fate or persons cannot be controlled, addiction to substances or addiction to substance abusers.

Maybe the simplest way to think of co-dependency and life scripts is to merge them under a single label, the co-dependent script, recognizing that . . .

1. Co-dependency and maladaptive life scripts are a consequence of upbringing in a dysfunctional family system.

2. Both have a repetitive pattern. One of the surest
   indicators of a self-defeating life script is a series of
   unhappy situations that regularly repeat themselves: the
   woman who marries three alcoholics in a row, the
   abstinent alcoholic who tragically thinks he can go back
   to "social drinking" a second, third or fourth time.
3. Both have negative influences on the course of adult life.
   Undue stress, anxiety, unhappy relationships,
   unsatisfying careers, excitement addiction, boredom or
   failure to "get a kick out of life" are some of the common
   marks of either co-dependency or a maladaptive life
   script.
4. In both cases self-limiting belief systems restrict options
   for living by choice. Risk-taking may be limited to either
   fear of failure or fear of success.
5. Both co-dependents and those who live out their lives
   with a maladaptive script tend to deny their
   responsibility for their lot in life.
6. Both are lacking in the power of will, the translation of
   positive desire into appropriate action. Compulsively
   dependent on others for solutions to life's problems,
   co-dependents are short on motivation or the "get up and
   go" to take charge of their destiny.

Unless they make decisions in favor of autonomy, co-dependents continue through life as victims, bound to their
scripts and the unconscious influence of their negative childhood programming.

Breaking Through Denial

Freedom from bondage to a co-dependent script begins with
self-discovery, of thinking in terms of the adage "Know thyself."

For a moment think of what it means to be inner-directed, to
be in charge of your thoughts, feelings, perceptions and actions.
It might seem scary at first to think of yourself as being fully
responsible for your life, but do it anyway. Think *power*, the kind
of power that comes with self-confidence and faith in your
ability to learn the coping skills others have learned.

Escaping your co-dependency calls for information about
what you are breaking free from, some knowledge of how you

got to be the way you are. Think of your life as a play and yourself as the author. Is your script a portrayal of happiness, of good struggling with evil or of doom and an aimless odyssey? Is it a comedy, a farce, a tragedy, a romance or simply the report of one who goes through life barely getting by? Think of yourself as a drama critic and in a phrase or sentence write a theme for your script. Make it short and to the point. For example . . .

- Life's a struggle anyway, so what's the use of trying?
- Everything always comes up roses for me.
- I was born to carry a burden all my life.
- Try hard, but don't succeed.
- My rewards will come in heaven.
- Mama's little helper.
- Nice guys always lose.
- Might as well be dead (crazy) than be this way.
- Someday my ship will come in.
- Born to lose.

People's speech often reveals their script theme. Fred spent 14 years in prison for being an accomplice to a murder. A naive, co-dependent kid, he simply "went along with the gang" on a joyride, never guessing it would end up in robbery and a killing. Over and over in his recovery group, Fred would say, "Man, I'm born dead." In abstinence he lived a life without life in it.

How would you describe the character you've mainly played so far in life? Have you been the star of your show or little more than a supporting character? Who have you felt you had to play second fiddle to and what have you thought about that? Who have you had to please or whose approval have you had to win to play your part according to your script?

Just as a play is fiction so is the belief that people-pleasing is the only route to successful living. Many of us, as we examine the nature of our scripts and the players we chose for it, discover we are living out an illusion. The people and events on which our scripts were based have physically passed out of our lives, but we have kept them psychologically alive in our minds and reacted to their ghostly presence as if they still controlled our destiny. Identifying these power players in your script can make it easier to rewrite your script and make yourself the star.

Winners Or Losers

If your play went on the road today, would you get top billing or just be a member of the cast? When the curtain comes down, will you be a Winner, a Loser, or simply an In-Betweener, one who's played out life in plain old, everyday-variety unhappiness?

Being an In-Betweener is a lot of what co-dependency is all about. We exist as neither Winners nor Losers. We get by but the joy of winning on a regular basis passes us by. Some of us are Almost Winners, but every time it looks as if we'll come out on top, we sabotage our shot at success by acting out our co-dependency. Some of us are Almost Losers. With little more than perseverance we manage to hang in there as survivors. There are also those who won't hang on to their abstinence and fall through the cracks into the ranks of the real Losers. For most of us, though, life's an unpleasant roller coaster until and unless we decide to get off and change our life script.

What values have you reflected as you've played your part in this play? Good or evil? Weak or strong? Noble or petty? Grandiosity or humility? Scrooge or Good Samaritan? Robber Baron or Robin Hood? Wicked Witch or Florence Nightingale? What have you showed your audience that you stood for as you've acted your part in the drama (or lack of it) in your life?

What emotions have you shown the world as you played your part? How do these play-acting emotions differ from the feelings you've felt in the "real you" as you went about acting out your script?

One thing co-dependents do very well is hide their real selves and feelings behind the mask that fits the character they choose to be at any given moment. They cloak their anger behind a smile and commit emotional dishonesty. They hide behind an Iron Mask, paying the price in physical afflictions or emotional and spiritual dis-ease.

Highlighting the difference between our real feelings and those we choose to show the world emphasizes our co-dependency with that world. When we hide ourselves from others we link ourselves to those we choose to hide from. The more open, honest and autonomous we become, the more we move away from co-dependency and progress toward self-dependency.

What is the conflict that moves your plot toward its climax? What obstacles must be overcome? How does your play end? What will life be like for you in five or ten years if you stick with the script you are playing out now? Are you destined for winning, losing or only getting by?

As you consider the relevance between life scripts and individual destiny, be reminded again of the probability that the script you are living by today is one you decided on as a child. Reacting to your survival needs in a dysfunctional family, you chose your way of being in the world without knowing what life was like in a reasonably well-adjusted family. You lacked the information needed to create a script to achieve comfortable living and close relationships.

Looking at your script now and evaluating how it has worked offers you the opportunity to rewrite it, keeping what is good in it and throwing out the bad. You have the chance now to write your own script, to be your own director and put your name up in lights as the star of the show.

Roles People Play In Life

To think along the lines of digging and discovering is a way to get some idea of your life directions and how they have been affected by your co-dependent script. Examining the roles you've played is a specific approach to choice-making. How appropriate to your own well-being has it been to act like someone you haven't really wished to be? How has it worked for you to pretend to be what you were not? How have you felt while always waiting for someone else to make the first move, always waiting to know which way the wind blew before you dared assert yourself?

The transactional analysis people see three dominant roles people play as they live out their life scripts. They are *Victim, Persecutor* and *Rescuer.* To help you better identify these roles and how they affect the lives of co-dependents, here are some key elements of each:

Victims

Victims feel victimized. They feel put upon by fate or others. They do not see themselves as responsible for whatever misery befalls them. They blame the circumstances of their childhoods, their sex, their religion, their education or lack of it, their ethnic roots or the stars for their misfortunes.

Victimhood cannot necessarily be judged by appearance or material means. The I. Magnin lady driving a Jaguar and married to a physically abusive doctor is a co-dependent Victim. The tough-talking truckdriver who feels suicidal because he is repeatedly "taken to the cleaners" by his lady friends is a co-dependent Victim. The chief executive officer of a Fortune 500 company who feels he "just lucked out" in the corporate world and fears his peers will recognize him as a phony is a co-dependent Victim. Victims are more the captive of their scripts than they are of the circumstances of their adult lives. They go on reliving the one-down position they suffered in childhood, hoping some "one" or some "thing" will rescue them from victimhood.

Persecutors

Persecutors persecute. They attack, nag, criticize and in general project the attitude that they are right and everyone else is wrong. Persecutors are aggressive co-dependents who mask their vulnerability and lack of self-regard behind an air of superiority. They deny their feelings of being "less than" by assuming a position of being "better than." The illusion of power that goes with 'persecuting' provides protection against their fear of abandonment or the pain of their isolation.

I grew up with two Persecutors as role models. Sarcasm was considered humor and criticism dominated the daily conversation. In selling I learned that sarcasm was simply not the way to influence people and win customers. It took a lot of work and a lot of time to give up the sarcasm that I learned in childhood.

Rescuers

Rescuers rescue, whether asked to or not. Some are influenced by aphorisms such as, "It is nobler to give than to receive" and "You are your brother's keeper." Others simply took up the habit of rescuing because there was no one else to do it in their dysfunctional families.

In early life rescuing provides more good feelings than suffering victimization or persecuting others. In later life though, both professional and amateur rescuers frequently burn out. Life goes flat for them as they become victims of their own scripts.

Switching Roles

Victims, Persecutors and Rescuers suffer a common need for involuntary interaction with others. They are driven to fulfill their roles. A choice of roles is beyond their grasp until they recognize the nature of their co-dependency, the negative consequences of it and their compulsive need to always be in control of others.

Few people constantly cling to a single role. They switch from Persecutor to Victim, Rescuer to Persecutor, or maybe Victim to Rescuer. This switching around is essential to the games we play and the acting-out of our life scripts.

Here's an example of how this flip-flopping from one role to another works:

A Captain-of-the-Fleet type demands a spit-and-polish atmosphere in his home and in doing so closes himself off from intimacy and family love. Justifying his role of Perennial Persecutor, he righteously insists, "The right way is the Navy way."

His wife sticks to her Victim role but occasionally tires of his nagging and flies into a rage, then switches into *her* Persecutor role and makes her husband a Victim. Susy, the youngest daughter and peacekeeper in this dysfunctional family, steps in as a Rescuer and attempts to calm the turmoil. But she suddenly becomes a Victim as both parents turn on her and shout, "Butt out! Mind your own business."

Sometimes, if Susy plays the Victim role hard enough and spills enough tears, Father tries to be a Rescuer by buying her a new dress. Then Mother, in the privacy of the bedroom where she fights her many battles, jumps on Father and shrills, "There you go again . . . spoiling her."

In time they all settle back into their most familiar roles and peace prevails until their life scripts demand another switch.

Imagine a triangle with each angle labeled Persecutor, Rescuer or Victim. At one time or another each of us unconsciously moves around this psychological triangle and changes roles as circumstances warrant. Professionally this is known as the "Karpman triangle" which establishes, as Stephen Karpman wrote, "There is no drama unless there is a switch in the roles." (4)

This switching provides excitement in life and is inherent to the role-playing dynamics Eric Berne described in *Games People Play*. Games are forms of self-defeating human interactions that provoke an illusion of close connection with others. The games of co-dependency are a constant source of bad feelings that adversely affect the quality of life for the co-dependent as they inhibit the human potential for healthy relationships. (More on games in the next chapter.)

Role Identification

Freedom from co-dependency calls for breaking away from the triangle, abandoning old roles and the game-playing that goes with them. The first step you can take in this direction is to identify the roles you play most often in your interactions with others. Simply knowing when you are acting like a Persecutor, Victim or Rescuer is a tremendous step forward on the road of self-discovery. Knowing the patterns of verbal and vocal expression, language and feelings that accompany the varied roles will help you know what you want to "change from" as you begin the process of "changing to" a more self-dependent person. Here are some clues to help you in your task of self-discovery:

Verbal Clues

Persecutors tend to dictate "You should" or "You ought to." They say "You always" and "You never" a lot. They criticize and nit-pick.

Victims say "I wish" "Why me?" "If only" and "Why does this always happen to me?" They blame others. They avoid yes and no answers and rarely speak in clear terms. They invite criticism from Persecutors by saying, "I guess so" or "You know" regularly.

Rescuers say things like, "I'm only trying to help you" or "That's too bad. Let me show you how to do that." "There, there, everything will be all right" is a Rescuer term.

Vocal Tones

Persecutors speak in harsh tones. They try to demonstrate power by vocal force. They bark like Army sergeants or express irritation in their vocal tones.

Victims may plead or whine. Their voices are often flat or dead, expressing their feelings of helplessness or hopelessness.

Sometimes they may come across as too exuberant or enthusiastic and invite scorn or rejection by others.

Rescuers usually sound warm, nurturing and supportive. However, sometimes their verbal and vocal expressions don't match. They may say, "I'm only trying to help . . . " but their vexation betrays them and they sound more like a Persecutor than a Rescuer.

Body Language

Persecutors frown and jut their jaw forward. They jab at people with their forefinger and pound tables. They want to give the appearance of being in charge or Top Dog in the game of life.

Victims slump. They drag themselves around. They rarely smile. In conversation their hands wander around a lot, gesturing a message of powerlessness.

Rescuers smile and chuckle quite a bit. They pat people on the shoulder and do a lot of hugging.

Feeling Clues

Persecutors have many feelings of anger and often confuse power with confidence. Feelings of irritation cover their sense of frustration because others don't or won't do things "right."

Victims feel helpless and hopeless. Some say they just feel "wasted away" with the feelings of not being able to assert themselves or be in charge of their lives. They tend to feel overly grateful when given a hand by others.

Rescuers may have different feelings as they act out their roles. Sometimes they have the warm, good feeling of helping others and being a caring, nurturing person. Other times they may feel martyrdom, so put upon by others they are actually victimized by those they hope to rescue. The feelings then can be resentment, anger or a stoic resignation, the "Joan of Arc" feelings that come to those who feel they sacrifice themselves for others.

Knowing what role you are in at any given time and set of circumstances paves the way for making choices. You can choose to play Persecutor, Victim or Rescuer if appropriate. For example:

A mother decides, "No TV for you kids 'til you get your homework done." (Persecutor)

An employee who needs his job thinks, "I hate the way they treat us here but there's nothing I can do about it." (Victim)

A bank loan officer says to a delinquent creditor, "Okay, you've always been on time with your payments in the past. I could get into trouble with my boss but I'll give you 30 more days to get caught up." (Rescuer)

Making appropriate choices is an exercise in autonomy. Choosing a role rather than unconsciously "playing" one is letting go of co-dependency and demonstrating self-dependency.

Do's And Don'ts That Haunt Our Minds

As a co-dependent there is little likelihood you've made it through life this far without suffering some strong feelings about certain things you should or shouldn't do. They make up the *Do's* and *Don'ts* imprinted in your childhood programming. Both consciously and unconsciously they affect your way of being in the world, your work, your friendships and your relationships. They are a sample of the values of your family. They can be stated in brief phrases such as the following:

Do go to school.
Do get a job.
Do go to church.
Do get married.
Do save money.
Do improve yourself.
Do be somebody. (Businessman, priest, doctor, lawyer, etc.)

This is a short list. There are many more *Do's* that influence our lives. They reflect the expectations of all those we looked up to as children. They are the "shoulds" that push us in our desires to get certain things out of life. When we accomplish them, we feel good. When we don't, we feel bad.

Time after time in growth workshops, people talk about all the things they "should" have done in life and their guilt or depression because they failed to do so. Even though they might be quite successful, they feel they somehow failed to be what they were "supposed" to be or do what they were "supposed" to do.

Derek was well on his way to success as a writer. He felt a strong urge to get a college degree to enhance his opportunities and reputation. Nobody in his family had ever attended college and he felt he "ought to," even though he admitted that the writing field is notorious for successes who've never gone to college. After he realized he was pleasing "them" instead of pleasing himself, he decided to stick with his writing rather than being detoured four years in college. He now does a syndicated feature, writes books and articles for writers and leads seminars for them, has a ready market for his books and feels good about his future.

And then there are the *Don'ts*, the less easily identified messages that keep us from doing what we want to do or hinder us in our pursuit of successful living. In milder forms they serve as cautions against our impulsiveness. "Don't make waves" can be prudent advice to go slow in certain circumstances. But in severe dependency, a deeply imprinted "Don't make waves" message can result in painful timidity or shyness.

Do messages are usually delivered to a child in verbal form. They can also be demonstrated by a parent as examples of what they want or expect a child to do or become in adulthood. Mommy is a nurse, is happy and says, "Do be a nurse." By word of mouth and by attitude and action she "walks her talk," so Sally grows up to be a happy nurse.

Dad says, "Do be a nurse." He's not a nurse. He thinks of nursing as "woman's work" and just wants Betty to have a vocation in case she doesn't find a husband. Betty grows up and fulfills her father's expectations but in a few years is an unhappy nurse. Her life is ruled more by a *Don't* message, "Don't be happy."

Parents send many mixed messages. They don't always say what they mean or do what they say they're doing. The result is confusion and conflict in the messages recorded in any child's memory bank. Some of these mixed-up messages, the *Do* ones and the *Don't* ones, are reflections of the craziness of a dysfunctional family or of the conflicting messages in the mind of a dysfunctional parent.

Do's As Drivers

Many of the *Do's* programmed into our belief systems are benign. They are mild reminders that certain behaviors brought us affection and approval in childhood.

In the ordinary process of maturing as adults we usually
come to realize the world we live in is not the world our
parents lived in. In adulthood, we find some of the *Do's* that
made sense to our parents are not appropriate for us. We are
not the children we once were.

Nevertheless, some of us remain so tightly bound to these
Do's that they negatively influence our life performance as
adults. Even though our experience may dictate otherwise, we
cling to the illusion that if we satisfy these long-outdated parental demands and do what they wanted us to do, our lives will be
okay. The *Do's* unconsciously drive us toward compliance even
though our conscious mind tells us they push us toward mental
turmoil and/or physical collapse.

Transactional analysts Taibi Kahler and Hedges Capers identified these compelling *Do's* as "drivers" and list five of them.
The parenthetical interpretations are mine:

- Do be perfect. (I'll never be good enough.)
- Do try hard. (I guess I'll never get to the top.)
- Do please me. (I just can't do enough to please you.)
- Do hurry up. (I'm going as fast as I can.)
- Do be strong. (I'm afraid to show my feelings.) (5)

Behind all these "drivers" is the unconscious fear that failure
to carry them out will bring rejection and abandonment. These
fears negatively affect the quality of our well-being. Until we
accept ourselves as we are and make choices for change, we
cling to the intellectual, emotional and behavioral habits that go
with our co-dependent scripts.

- The perfectionists are driven toward perfection but suffer
  the pain of knowing they will never be perfect enough.
- The strivers are driven to try hard instead of winning
  while continuing their commitment to the deepseated belief
  that life's a struggle.
- The people-pleasers are driven to sacrifice their needs in
  the illusory hope that pleasing others will bring its own
  rewards.
- The hurriers are driven to rush through life, never knowing what it means to slow down and smell the flowers.

• The stoics are driven to deny the need for healthy emotional expression and their need for close connections with
others.

All of these "drivers" reflect our relationship with ourselves
and are a part of the "stage business" that goes with acting out
our life scripts. All of them can be modified and their intensity
reduced once we start living in the present and taking responsibility for what we do, the way we do it and the pace at which
we do it.

You have the power of choice to change. Before deciding
what to change it is important to understand something of the
Don'ts and injunctions that sabotage our best intentions and
undermine our efforts at changing from co-dependence to self-
dependence.

Don'ts As Stoppers

There are always "stoppers" in our life scripts, that bar or
detour us from the path we perceive as the route to successful
living. Have you ever had the feeling that some mysterious
something is holding you back in life, keeping you from the
achievement of your dreams? Maybe you've set some rational
goal for yourself but somehow you just don't get the necessary
things done to meet that goal. Your mind is tortured, your sleep
disturbed, you see yourself as "less than" and you feel guilty as
you fritter away time that you know you "should" be using
more productively.

It's as though our actions are dictated by a subliminal message
flashing on the screen in our mind: "Don't, Don't, Don't." These
Don'ts are injunctions, "a prohibition or negative command from
a parent." (6) Incorporated into our childhood belief systems,
they continue to affect our adult lives adversely unless we decide
for ourselves the way we want our lives to go.

Stuck in joyless abstinence, a major turning point for me
came when I learned about injunctions, how to track them
down and how to redecide my life directions. Recognizing my
injunctions as creatures harbored in my mind helped me understand I could be the person I chose to be.

Most of my learning about that process went on with Bob
and Mary Goulding at the Western Institute for Group and

Family Therapy. In their book *The Power Is In The Patient* they list
13 injunctions:

> Don't be.
> Don't be a child.
> Don't make it.
> Don't be important.
> Don't belong.
> Don't grow.
> Don't.
> Don't be close.
> Don't be well (or sane).
> Don't be you (the sex you are).
> Don't think. (Don't think about X [forbidden subject]).
> Don't feel (Don't feel [mad, sad, glad, etc.]).
> Don't feel what you feel ([Feel what I feel]). (7)

Exploring with the Gouldings the childhood history long-
forgotten in my memory bank led me to the core issues of my
co-dependent script:

> Don't make it. (Why don't you do anything right?)
> Don't be important. (You'll never be as smart as I am
>   [stepfather].)
> Don't belong. (Shame of poverty and inadequacy.)
> Don't be close. (No hugs, kisses or intimacy.)
> Don't show your feelings. (Machismo.)

These *Don'ts* were a surrendering of my natural self to the
expectations of those who controlled my childhood development. This is not to blame them. They just treated me as they'd
been treated in childhood. They handed down the family rules
that had governed their childhood and been written into their
life scripts.

My stepfather, probably rebelling against the authoritarianism of his Lutheran minister father, acted out his aggressive co-
dependency with an air of superiority. He exemplified the working stiff's dream by letting the boss know, "You can take this job
and shove it."

Mother spent her life fighting off the "One Down" position women were expected to play in the days of her girlhood, the late 1890s and early part of the twentieth century. One of her drives was to be successful and economically independent. Her "Do try hard" message was so intense, the stress drove her twice into an emotional collapse.

These *Don'ts*, formulated in childhood, restrict the adult potential for personal growth. They reflect decisions made by a child as a consequence of his dysfunctional parenting. They may have been delivered verbally, nonverbally or both.

Father says many times, "Don't talk back to me." Sometimes he reinforces it with a smack on the butt or even a beating.

Mother is nonresponsive. When confronted with a problem, she casts her glance upward as though imploring God's help, shrugs her shoulders and sighs.

The only conclusion a little kid can make is, "There's no use talking around here. Dad socks me if I do and Mother's never any help anyway."

The little kid's decision about that, though probably not framed in specific thoughts or words, is "Don't talk," or "Don't speak up." In adulthood this injunction makes it difficult or almost impossible to be assertive when appropriate. His inability to state his needs holds him back in his career and keeps him from involvement in friendly or loving relationships with others. One of the benefits of self-help recovery groups is that they offer "Don't talkers" the chance to discover it can be safe to speak up in the presence of others.

Do's And Don'ts In Conflict

Most of us have *Do's* and *Don'ts* that tug us in different directions and result in self-sabotage. For example, "Do be perfect" is a common message but an impossible dream. It is also a way of reinforcing a "Don't make it" injunction and the stress that accompanies a *Do/Don't* conflict.

Tracking down his life script history in a workshop, a participant told of crazy driving habits on the freeway in his efforts to arrive at work on time. He was a "compulsive punctual." He was asked, "When you were a little kid, what happened when you were late or didn't get things done on time?"

Slapping his hand on his forehand he said, "Jeeesus. My dad had a fit. Bawled me out. Said he'd whip me. It was crazy."

"So for you being late is really scary?"

"Yeah." He had the look of a frightened boy.

"You're willing to risk your life to make your daddy happy?"

He shook his head from side to side, thought a minute, then said, "Hell, no. That'd be insane. He's dead seven years now."

Someone in the group said, "Sounds crazy to me."

Silence reigned momentarily. He looked around the group, then looked at me with the clear look that signals a moment of truth and said, "I'm not gonna die on the freeway trying to satisfy my dad."

Recognizing that his "Do be punctual (perfect)" urges had become self-defeating compulsive behavior led the way to a new decision for him. He decided to leave for work a little earlier every day and get on with becoming a Winner. The last I heard of him he was a successful electronic data processing consultant, a business in which he set his own hours. He'd broken out of his double bind, the impasse that existed in between his "Do be perfect" driver and his "Don't make it" injunction.

The *Do* drivers imply you have the personal power to competently manage your life course. They ignore the reality that co-dependency diminishes personal power and inhibits your potential for successful self-management. The paradox is that the co-dependent has a series of motivators — *Do* messages — and a conflicting series of demotivators — *Don't* messages. The consequence is an ongoing battle between the *Do's* and *Don'ts* which leads to discontent, a troubled mind or a stress-related illness. This *Do/Don't* struggle cheats you of mental and physical energy that might be better used in pursuit of successful living.

It's likely that at times in your life you have felt caught in this double bind between your *Do's* and *Don'ts*. You felt you wanted to do something but your Inner Saboteur provided a thousand reasons why you shouldn't. Your heart called for action but logic opted in favor of the status quo. The voices in your head said, "Don't rock the boat. Don't make waves." So you gave up and suffered all the bad feelings that go with giving up. Maybe you've even recognized a pattern of these *Do/Don't* contradictions that cheat you of the serenity spoken of so much in 12-Step programs.

However you got into the double binds of co-dependency, one thing for certain is that in reading this book you are at least thinking of resolving the conflicts of your co-dependent script. You are beginning to re-identify yourself and *see yourself as you are, rather than as you think you are supposed to be.* You may be approaching the breakthrough point seen many times in redecision workshops. Participants arrive at a new awareness and say, "Hey. I don't have to be like that any more. I don't have to follow that old script all my life."

Which, of course, is right. You don't have to be the way you were. You have the power of choice. All things are possible for those willing to let go of the past, make changes in the present and take positive action for the future.

Emotional Bondage To The Past

Emotions are links in a chain that bind us to our childhood programming. The feelings of childhood are not automatically left behind as we grow up. We gradually learn to stifle the expression of our emotions in order to conform to the family rules about them. We make a habit of "keeping cool" in the hope we will be loved or accepted by those who make the rules. We arrive at adulthood with the injunction "Don't feel" strongly embedded in our belief systems.

As grownups it just doesn't occur to most of us that we can be responsible for the feeling habits that influence our moods and behaviors. Bob Goulding says, " . . . each person is really in charge of himself, but he has been persuaded by most of the people around him that he is not. Our songs, our folklore, our literature repeatedly insist, that the world makes me feel bad, or good, or sad, or angry." (8)

In childhood we were the victims of our experience. Lacking information, we accepted our world (family) as normal and all those in higher authority as speakers of the Truth. When they defined our identity and told us how to feel, most of us let ourselves be molded just as wet clay is molded onto the potter's wheel. And just as the product of the potter's wheel can reflect the imperfections of the potter, so can the product of parenting reflect the imperfections of the parent.

One imperfection of parents is the projection of their own dysfunctional feeling habits onto their children. Unable or unwilling to "own" their responsibility for anger, guilt, depression or bad feelings in general, they project them onto their children.

They send subliminal messages that somehow the child is responsible for the parents' feelings. They say things like:

"You make me so angry when you don't mind."
"It makes Mama happy when you're such a good girl."
"You know it makes Daddy mad when you bully your
    brother."
"You'll be the death of me yet."
"You give me a headache."
"Don't argue with your mother. You know it makes her feel
    bad (sick) when you talk back."

There are three powerful dynamics involved in each of those
statements:

1. They are guilt-producing directives. Their purpose is the
   exercising of control by guilt. They are triggered by
   actions that fail to meet the expectations of others.
2. They promote the illusion that adults are not responsible
   for their feelings and that a child has a magical power to
   "make" others feel mad, sad, bad or glad.
3. They encourage the development of other-directedness
   in the self.

Here are some similar statements repeated but with a fourth
dynamic added — shame:

"You rotten kid. You make me so angry when you don't
    mind."
"It makes Mama so happy when you are a good girl. If
    there wasn't something wrong with you, you'd make
    Mama happy all the time."
"There must be some kind of devil in you the way you bully
    your brother and make Daddy mad."
"Shame on you. You'll be the death of me yet."
"If it weren't for you, I wouldn't have all these headaches."
"Satan's got your tongue or you wouldn't talk back to your
    mother like that and make her sick."

These shame-producing messages are more poisonous than
the guilt-producing ones. Guilt is a bad feeling about one's *actions*.

Shame is a bad feeling about one's very *being*. It is something we feel when we perceive, as Charles Whitfield writes, ". . . . that a part of us is defective, bad, incomplete, rotten, phoney, inadequate, or a failure." (9)

Each of these parent-child transactions provokes certain feelings depending on the child involved. The one bit of autonomy retained by a child is the right to choose, consciously or unconsciously, how he or she will react to the world.

The daily arguments in my own family drove my brother into retreat and passive co-dependency, me into combat and aggressive co-dependency. He was the Scapegoat and I the Hero in our family system. We were both subjected to the same unstable, combative environment but decided on different ways to cope with it. It challenged me into a fight mode, believing I was welcome in the fray. It drove him into a flight mode, believing nobody would listen to him anyway.

This pattern continued with us into adulthood just as it does with all co-dependents (except those who by chance or by choice manage to achieve a comfortable emotional maturity). With feelings stuffed down beyond the point of awareness, we frequently live an illusion of emotional maturity. We confuse our image with the self we have learned to mask.

Having bought into the popular conception that anything less than "keeping our cool" is inappropriate to being an adult, we often become a literal "walking time bomb." When the pressure of pent-up emotions reaches its blowing point, the consequences are unpredictable for us and everyone around us.

This is especially true when we find abstinence is no more than a bare-bones survival, barren of the joy and serenity so often dreamed of by those who've managed to wrench themselves free from chemical abuse. Long accustomed to avoiding the pain of self-contained conflict with mind-altering chemicals or compulsive behaviors, we don't know how to keep our emotional balance. We often misapply the power of our will in efforts to keep control over our feelings rather than learn how to express them. We store up these bad feelings, this emotional garbage, like pack rats.

Only when our well-being is sufficiently disrupted do we consider getting rid of the garbage. In time our only choice for increased well-being is to learn to deal with this emotional garbage. Letting go of old bad-feeling habits is crucial to supplanting them with good ones.

Recognizing the "feeling connnections" that link us with in-junctions, the *Don'ts* our parents taught us, is an essential step toward being fully in charge of our feeling habits. Recognizing those connections helps in putting a label on our emotions. Sharon Wegscheider-Cruse says, "Feelings that cannot be named cannot be talked about." (10) And "talking about" is fundamental to the therapeutic process of recovery.

Nevertheless, it can be difficult to acknowledge that feelings learned in childhood might be governing the course of our adult lives. Though it may not make sense on a rational basis, the reality is that re-experiencing the emotions of childhood without knowing what is going on can keep us stuck in an impasse of unhappiness.

On some unconscious level outside of our awareness, we fear defiance of the rules laid down for us in childhood. We fear that we might have to relive old fears of physical and emotional pain or the terror of abandonment. Unaccustomed to the concept of being responsible for our feelings, thoughts and actions, we fear walking on and taking charge of our destiny.

As you increase your understanding of injunctions and the fears that go with them, you take the first step toward discon-necting yourself from emotional bondage. The following short sampling may help you identify the injunctions and fears that continue to affect you in your present life:

- Don't make it (fear of success).
- Don't be you (fear of being yourself).
- Don't feel (fear of showing feelings).
- Don't be a child (fear of spontaneity or fun).
- Don't be close (fear of intimacy).

Warning! As you consider this matter of injunctions and bad feelings, don't dwell on the negative. Instead think of the won-derful opportunities for successful living that lie ahead as you start living by autonomous choice rather than by co-dependent thinking and feeling habits. Digging around in your feelings may be more painful than exploring your thought process but, as they say around recovery circles, "No short-term pain, no long-term gain."

Degrees Of Co-dependency

Co-dependency is not an either/or matter. There is no clear-cut line between co-dependency and nonco-dependency. Co-dependency is a matter of degree: mild, moderate, severe. Just as combat veterans of the Vietnam conflict have suffered the aftereffects of their experience in varying degrees, so can children raised in an alcoholic or otherwise dysfunctional family system suffer their co-dependency in varying degrees as an aftereffect of their childhood experience.

You can easily check this out for yourself. Are you more comfortable around some people than with others? Do you feel more comfortable in some situations than in others? Do you feel more inclined to agree with some people than with others, even though you may hold a differing view? Does your OK-ness depend on the clothes you wear, the car you drive or the person you love or live with?

Having some idea as to the degree of your co-dependency can be helpful in considering a growth or treatment plan meant to move you on toward autonomy. Deciding whether your co-dependency is mild, moderate or severe is a matter of self-discovery. And self-discovery calls for some examination of yourself in relationship to the way others identify and cope with their co-dependency. Doing so is a part of the analytical task necessary to know who you are and where you want to go from here. It may be difficult but, as Eric Berne wrote, "Self-analysis is like giving oneself a haircut: with sufficient care and practice it can be done." (11)

Whatever you do as you examine the intensity of your co-dependency, go to some meetings of Co-dependents Anonymous (CoDA). There you will hear stories of the ways co-dependency has affected the lives of others. You can check yourself out on how you stand compared to others. And you may hear some who have been abstainers for years but whose co-dependency unknowingly stood between them and happiness until they began dealing with it as an issue separate from their addiction.

Primary And Secondary Co-dependency

Having recognized yourself as a co-dependent to some degree, the next step is determining the difference between primary

and secondary co-dependency. This is another way of saying
what is included in the reading of the Preamble at every Co-
dependents Anonymous meeting: "The only requirement for
membership is a desire for healthy and fulfilling relationships
with others and ourselves."

Primary co-dependency concerns the relationship you have with
yourself and how you think and feel about yourself. It is a state
of being victimized by the programming of the past. It reflects
a toxic belief system and perpetuates an illusion of inadequacy
and incompetency arising from the negative influences of a
dysfunctional family. In its severest form it is at the far end of
the scale away from autonomy.

Moving from primary co-dependency toward autonomy calls
for changes in the co-dependent script and the roles played to
sustain it. How to do that will be further discussed in chapters
six and nine.

Secondary co-dependency concerns your relationships with others. It is a source for the negative thinking/feeling payoffs that
go with unhealthy "people-connections." It is a continuation of
dysfunctional communication habits learned in childhood. It reflects the fear we have of being ourselves and the avoidance of
openness and honesty in our transactions with others.

Changing from secondary co-dependency to healthy, fulfilling
relationships calls for giving up the "games people play" and getting on with new habits of listening and interacting with others.

Some people begin their recovery by tackling primary co-
dependency first. Some go after secondary recovery first, hoping improved relationships with others will bring an improved
relationship with self. That's how I started out. However, along
the way I found I had to change *me* before I could make much
beneficial change in my relationships with others.

Maybe it doesn't really matter which way you choose to begin
your recovery from a flawed life script and co-dependency.
What matters most is getting started. Walk on. Somewhere
along the way you will find freedom from others' expectations
and the joy of being yourself.

❦ 3 ❧

Games
Co-dependents Play

For certain fortunate people there is something which transcends all classifications of behavior, and that is awareness; something which arises above the programming of the past, and that is spontaneity; and something that is more rewarding than games, and that is intimacy.

— **Eric Berne, MD**

Somewhere it is written, "When the student is ready, the teacher will appear." That's how it was with me in the late 1960s when I came across *Games People Play* and Eric Berne's idea that the analysis of human interactions could be a practical tool for those of us seeking a path to recovery. Berne's tools point the way to liberating ourselves from past programming and the terrible bonds of self-defeating attitudes and actions.

Berne's translation of psychiatric knowledge into popular language introduced me to a new self-awareness. I began to realize I might be responsible for the anguish I was experiencing in my abstinence. It has long been said that "One picture is worth a thousand words," and Berne's diagrams outlining the basic dynamics of transactional analysis proved that adage true for me. This experience of stumbling on such a clear and simple explanation of my life and behavior proved to be a powerful motivator for me to continue on the path of self-discovery. Since then I have introduced hundreds of others to these tools in my classes and workshops.

You certainly, at one time or another in your life, have thought or said, "Now why did I say that?" Troubled by bad feelings in the aftermath of some effort at communication with another, you may have racked your brain and tortured yourself wondering what went wrong. Maybe you've also wondered, "Why does this happen over and over?"

If this rings a bell for you, this chapter can help you gain helpful insight into your own game-playing and how it fosters co-dependency.

Games

Though the word "co-dependency" does not show up in Berne's writings on transactional analysis, his concept of "games" graphically portrays the communication styles of co-dependent interactions with others. What exactly are these games? For our purposes here we'll define them as "go-no-where," time-wasting interactions which only reinforce co-dependency. They are operational habits learned in a dysfunctional family system. Though they may have served a function in surviving in childhood, when carried into adulthood, they inhibit the effectiveness of communication and stand in the way of open and honest interactions. The longing for intimacy that is so often the fate of co-dependents is the result of game-playing, which produces great distancing between people.

When communication styles learned in childhood are continued in adulthood, they bring with them the same bad feelings they did in much younger days. They provoke the same feelings of anger, irritation, frustration, guilt, depression, anxiety, helplessness, hopelessness, shame or suspicion suffered in childhood.

This return of familiar childlike feelings to the adult here-and-now is a function of "stimulus-response" reactions rather than a direct and open response to the present. A sticky situation in the present provokes a return to the past, echoing back the uncomfortable and sometimes agonized feelings of childhood. When *bad-feeling payoffs* come as a result of interactions with others, it is a sure sign you have been engaged in a game. Bad feelings consistently repeated in a relationship are evidence

of co-dependency at work. Autonomous or e
people change, modify or let go of games
freedom from bad feelings.

Something to keep in mind about "gamey'
many co-dependents have suppressed their c
so long they suffer "psychic numbness" or intellectualize instead
of feeling their feelings. If you "freeze up" in your efforts at
communication, regularly tend to "overexplain" to justify your
beliefs or actions, or know no emotion other than anger, it may
take some practice to recognize your *bad-feeling payoffs* and identify your games. Be patient. You don't get game-free overnight.

In my case, not realizing the extent to which my co-dependent
script influenced my relationships with others, I began my investigation of game-playing by analyzing the games other people
played. Having hidden behind an intellectual shield almost half
a lifetime, my growth came slowly as I gradually learned to feel
my feelings and recognize my own games. One of the things I
had to give up was my attitude of "I'm OK — You've messed
up," fostered in early childhood to cover up the low self-esteem
engendered by my feelings about our poverty and my earlier
abandonment to "boarding homes."

Of course, I have no way of knowing what's gone on in your
life or how it has affected your relationships with others. I do
know, however, that in the years I have been looking for an
easier, faster way of making constructive change in human
relationships, the finest tools I've found are the ones that come
in the TA toolkit.

Who Are The Adult, The Parent And The Child In TA?

*In the following pages I'll explore some of the key principles of
Transactional Analysis, sharing the roles of your Adult, who is the
mature you; your Parent, who gives you the nagging authoritarian
messages you received in childhood, and the Child, the frightened inse-
cure you who is still in need of strokes, nurturing and loving.*

Ulterior Transactions And Hidden Agendas

An ulterior transaction is "a transaction with a covert or
hidden message." (1) It is terribly difficult for little kids in a

...unctional family to be direct and honest with their parents. To do so is to invite negative feedback such as putdowns, scoldings or punishment.

Children thus learn to withhold their thoughts and feelings or be devious. They send their parents "sliders," messages in which their words mean one thing but their body language or vocal tone says something else. Betsy Lou agrees with her mother by saying, "Yes, Mommy, Auntie Jane is nice," but at the same time she shakes her head from side to side. Her body language contradicts her verbal message.

Feeling unable to directly state their needs or wants, they "beat around the bush" or hint at their desires. They send "crooked" messages, hoping to get what they want without the risks of confrontation. Many of these communication habits develop out of trial and error, others are learned directly from parents.

Here's an adult's "crooked" message: "Don't you think one drink after dinner is enough, dear? You really don't need those extra calories." The overt message is, "I'm concerned about your weight." The covert message, the hidden agenda, is, "I'm worried about your drinking." An upfront, honest message might have been: "Enough already. I'm not going to call your boss in the morning and make excuses for you."

Another "crooked" message might be, "I thought the doctor said you'd be giving up the Valium by now." An honest message might have been, "You really seem out of it a lot lately, honey. I'm worried you might be getting hooked on those pills."

Chances are you have been both a sender and receiver of thousands of "crooked" messages. You know what it means to want something, but either by habit or fear of a particular person or situation you attempt "diplomacy." You probably also know the feelings of resentment or anger that are triggered when you feel someone is trying to manipulate you with "crooked" messages.

Ulterior transactions and hidden agendas are the cornerstones of a co-dependent's communication style. It takes time and practice to send honest, objective messages without being brash and arrogant or subservient and submissive.

However, before you can overcome the habit of ulterior transactions, you first need to get straight with yourself. You need to be clear with the reality that you are responsible for your own game-playing. And you need to know something about the ways we set ourselves up for the bad-feeling rackets that perpetuate our co-dependency. Only when we can clearly see the games we play can we choose to live game-free lives.

Setting Yourself Up For Bad Feelings

Accepting personal responsibility for one's bad feelings is a complicated matter. Few of us, ignorant of the workings of our mind, are willing to admit that we set ourselves up to suffer feelings of guilt, resentment, fear, hurt, anger or all the feelings of worthlessness and inadequacy that go with low self-esteem.

Looks of puzzlement are the usual response when I ask people in workshops, "What is your favorite bad feeling?"

My next question is, "What bad feeling is the most familiar to you? What bad feeling do you have over and over? What is your usual feeling when things are difficult for you?"

At this point a light turns on for two or three in the group. They recognize that certain feelings consistently bother them. As they talk about these bad feelings they make a connection between certain feelings and certain situations. The word "always" slips into their conversation. They say things like:

"Mad. Angry. I *always* get angry when someone bosses
   me around."
"God. I don't know. I *always* get weak, like Jello, you know,
   powerless, when I get around people I think are better
   than me."
"I just freeze up. When someone challenges my knowledge
   about something, it seems like my mind *always* goes
   blank.
   I just get this silly grin on my face and try to act like
   everything's okay."

In a matter of minutes most people in the group will agree that they have certain bad feelings connected to threatening situations. With a little more prodding, they are able to recall that these were the feelings they had over and over again in their childhood.

Berne said, "When the patient is young, his parents teach him how to feel when things get difficult: In our family, when things get difficult, we feel guilty (afraid, hurt, angry, inadequate, baffled)." (2)

In adulthood these bad feelings reinforce our co-dependent scripts, our roles as Victims, Persecutors or Rescuers. They are the payoffs for our games and lead us to engage in "rackets." In rackets we trick or manipulate others into becoming our foils, responding to us in ways that "justify" the bad feelings that have become so familiar to us. We create self-deceptive illusions in which we can believe that someone else "made" us feel guilty, afraid, hurt, angry, inadequate, baffled; in this way we avoid responsibility for our own emotional well-being.

One way to check yourself out on "rackety behavior" is to ask yourself, "How did my mom or dad handle things when the going was rough?" Unless they were unusually calm and collected people, they probably modeled a wide variety of bad feelings: anger, confusion, depression, guilt, fear, nervousness or anxiety.

"If they did not usually respond with Adult action," say Paul McCormick and Leonard Campos, "they probably taught you a feeling racket." They say, "Most of your bad feelings are not 'for real.'" (3)

The question for you then, when suffering bad feelings, is to check out their authenticity. Are they appropriate to the present or are they repetitions of habits you learned from your parents? If they are not appropriate to the present, it is time for you to exercise your autonomy.

To be autonomous is to be free of rackets. When we recognize and take responsibility for the bad feelings we create for ourselves, we open the door to a relatively game-free life and true serenity.

Some Games Of Co-dependency

The first step toward a game-free life is to identify which games cause the greatest problems in your relationships. Once you have identified one or two of these games, you will have made the first step toward enjoying Win/Win relationships.

Look for the transactions that go on over and over in your life, ones that provoke bad feelings and are damaging to your well-being and relationships.

Be careful that you don't try to reduce all your interactions to game analysis. And don't be too hard on yourself as you become aware that you are largely responsible for your games. Instead give yourself some praise for the work you are doing right now to free yourself from the games and change your co-dependent script.

Games are played with varying degrees of intensity. There are "soft" game players and "hard" game players.

For example, Mac is fairly conscientious in his work as a receiving clerk. However, he plays "soft" self-effacing games. These attract negative attention, but not enough to be disastrous. From time to time he makes "attention-getting" mistakes in his paperwork or in routing supplies to their appropriate destinations.

His boss considers Mac about average but certainly not outstanding. The boss tells him, "Well, you know, Mac, you do okay for a while, then you screw up. Like routing those scalpels to the lab last week instead of to surgery."

Mac says, "Yeah, that was stupid." Then he grins. "For my pay, you know, I can't be perfect." He gives himself a back-handed putdown.

The boss only shrugs his shoulders. He has no idea why every so often Mac makes stupid mistakes. Knowing nothing of the dynamics of game-playing, it doesn't occur to Mac that when he messes up, he draws a lot of attention and there's some excitement for a while until things get straightened out. It's an old family scene with him, being replayed on the stage of adult life.

The Child in Mac is delighted even though the strokes he gets for these games of "Stupid" and "Kick Me" are negative and self-defeating. Frequently, he reinforces his game and his Victim role by laughing as he says, "There I go again. Why *do* I do such stupid things?" (To repeatedly laugh at one's own self-defeating behavior is an almost certain indication of a "gallows transaction," an interaction indicating gamey behavior and reinforcement of a Victim's script.) (4)

Mac doesn't use his Adult knowledge and ability to figure out that a little more competency would result in a better performance record and higher pay. Always feeling "less than," Mac doesn't think he deserves a better lot in life. When he does get a little praise he feels nervous about it and brushes it off just as he did in childhood. As an adult he simply doesn't recognize positive strokes, so he unconsciously sets himself up for negative strokes. Unless his "One Down" position gets too painful or boring to endure, he'll play out his lackluster script the rest of his life.

If Mac were to become more competent and self-confident, he would enjoy a higher level of self-esteem. If he gave up his game-playing, he would improve his relationship with his boss

and would move toward a game-free life. In either case, his
increased autonomy would free him from his Victim role and
facilitate his transition to a self-dependent person.

"Hard" game-players "go for broke." Without conscious intent
to do so, they literally put their lives on the line in the course of
their game-playing. Their payoffs include divorce, bankruptcy,
bad health, suicide or prison. This example comes from an Associated Press release:

> Mr. Anonymous was traveling cross-country via Amtrak and
> complained to officials his suitcase had been tampered with. They
> radioed ahead and police met them at the station. In the efforts to
> examine the suitcase for signs of tampering, it came open and the
> contents included 10 pounds and 11 ounces of cocaine.

Mr. Anonymous' "hard" games of "Stupid" and "Kick Me"
brought him negative strokes in the form of a prison term. The
negative payoff reinforced his Loser's life script and his role as
a Victim. Such behavior may not make sense but there is nothing sensible about hard game-playing. Losers are driven to
continue their dysfunctional behavior until they redecide their
life directions.

Now let's look at a few transactions easily recognized as
games and how they connect with co-dependency.

Victim Games

The game called "If It Weren't For Them" (you, him, her or
fate) is a blame-game. It symptomizes a perceived powerlessness
over individual destiny. It reflects an illusion that being blamed
can be avoided by blaming others.

Even in the healthiest of families it is natural for children to
attempt to escape responsibility by blaming others. In a dysfunctional family the cost for screwing up is so high that every
effort is made to weasel out of being blamed by those higher up
in the pecking order.

Unless the inclination to dodge blame by blaming others is
outgrown, it may become suppressed and its root cause forgotten. In adulthood, rather than feel the pain of being blamed, we
hide individual faults behind a screen of denial. "If It Weren't
For Them" players lose all concepts of self-responsibility. Instead

they put the blame on others just as they blamed brothers, sisters, teachers, or parents in childhood.

"Kick Me" is a game that epitomizes the unconscious way some of us set ourselves up for rejection or discounts. Even when it is staring them in the face it is very hard for some people to recognize how they contribute to self-defeating behavior. They make themselves scapegoats and play the role of Victim.

My earliest memories gave me a deep-seated conviction that I had to be "right." Listening to my mother and stepfather argue taught me it was terribly important to them that one would emerge as "right" and the other as "wrong."

For me, to be "wrong" made me a target for teasing and sarcasm from my stepfather. My perception of being wrong was that I was a failure and my fear of failure caused me to hang on to many attitudes and endeavors that were self-destructive or inappropriate.

It seemed an act of self-betrayal when I finally surrendered to the reality that what I perceived as "knowing what I was talking about," others saw as stubbornness and what I perceived as self-confidence, others saw as arrogance. Both attributes were part of a game of "Kick Me" that inhibited the quality of my relationships and cut me off from the kind of intimacy I now enjoy with my family.

"Kick Me" is a very common game among co-dependents, especially those who "hang in there" with an abusive mate. This game can be easily identified by watching a few *Laurel and Hardy* movies. It is not appropriate in real life for anyone to endure ongoing "scapegoating" as Laurel does. To do so is evidence of the severe co-dependency suffered by some people out of their desperate yearning for love and acceptance.

As in all games it takes two or more to play. "Kick Me" players often engage in provocative behavior to get their "kicks," putdowns or blows that reinforce the role of Victim and win for them the bad feelings of "Poor Me" that they seek. No one needs to live life on the short end of the stick just because that's the way it was in their childhood. No one has to stay a co-dependent. Anyone can choose to dance their own dance in life. They can give up their games of "Helpless" and make autonomous decisions to take charge of their lives.

Persecutor Games

"Now I've Got You, You Son Of A Bitch" (NIGYSOB) is a game easily recognized by anyone who repeatedly enters into what seems like ordinary communication only to be suddenly pounced upon. "NIGYSOB" players are out to prove their superiority through trapping Victims in an apparently innocent opening ploy or catching them in a violation of ambiguous "rules."

The ulterior motive of Persecutors is to feel "better than" the other person. They are completely unaware that the game-playing is a coverup for their low self-esteem. In this example of a "NIGYSOB" game the Spider (Persecutor) weaves his web and the Fly (Victim) gets caught:

> At a country-club dinner party the Persecutor says, "I imagine Sarah has an idea about that, don't you, Sarah? What do you think of the presidential campaign?" Sarah, flattered by her husband's attention, buys into the game. She says, "Well, it's pretty muddled right now. None of the candidates really say anything. They're just like kids calling each other names." Hubby Persecutor looks around the group. "That's Sarah for you. Typical female response. She never comes to grips with anything."
>
> Sarah is hurt, a familiar feeling for her, and clams up for the rest of the evening. Hubby feels triumphant and moves off to another group at the party to play his game of "NIGYSOB" and reinforce his feelings of superiority. Once again some other passive co-dependent will jump in to play the game, only to be left suffering in his wake.

"NIGYSOB" players and Persecutors often pride themselves on their "independence." They fail to recognize their co-dependency, their compulsive commitment to justifying their existence by "being right" and always being in control. Having gone this way myself for many years, I know with certainty it is a lonely road. When the false joy of "winning over others" fades away, the yearning for closer connections with other human beings can only be met by surrendering the co-dependent need for being in control of other people.

"Blemish" is a game played by those unwilling to accept themselves as they really are. They are unwilling to let themselves experience the feelings connected with their thoughts of inadequacy in childhood. They project their "blemishes" onto others.

The "Blemish" player is more direct than the "NIGYSOB" player. He doesn't go through any devious maneuvers before attacking. He nitpicks and criticizes, taking a false pride in his "honesty." He sends a lot of "you" messages:

"You burned my toast again." (The toast is only slightly darker than a golden tan.)

"You paid the light and water bill late." (He charged a new fishing rod to his Visa card because steelhead season was opening.)

"You didn't seem to get with it in bed last night." (He had too much to drink at the Fitch's anniversary party.)

"Blemish" players always attack to avoid any thought that they might be "less than." They are critical of everything and say, "Well, I don't expect anybody to be perfect but you (he, she, they) *should* do better than that." They are perfectionists in thought but not in deed. Rather than handle the "shoulds" and "ought to's" registered in their childhood programming, they project them on others. This anger at the perceived faults of others is really self-anger avoided by projecting it outside.

Considering the many traits associated with co-dependent relationships, there are few of us who have not played "Blemish" to one degree or another. My own awareness of it came 25 years ago in a meeting of recovering alcoholics.

Responding to one of my flashes of resentment at having to meet with "those people," someone said, "Look, buster, if we say anything here that makes you mad, go home and look in the mirror."

It took a long time for that to break through my barrier of denial. I didn't want to accept my anger at myself for being less than perfect. However, I slowly learned to recognize my anger at others as a symptom of the low self-esteem I'd long kept hidden from the world. Later, in redecision therapy, I connected my "Blemish" playing with my childhood rejection of constant criticism from my parents.

You can easily check out the extent of your "Blemish" playing. If you feel angry, resentful or irritated with others' faults, the chances are that you are temporarily getting rid of your own perceived inadequacies and projecting them onto others.

Once you recognize your projections you can use your new awareness of "Blemish" playing to your advantage. In *Born To Win* Muriel James and Dorothy Jongeward suggest you ask yourself this question when you become aware of your projections: "Could it possibly be true that trait really belongs to me?" (5)

Despite many resentments that are synonymous with early recovery, I took the advice given me so many years ago and did start looking in the mirror. It worked. Once I accepted responsibility for projecting my flaws onto others, I gave up (most of the time) conning myself into believing I had become the perfect person I was supposed to be.

Rescuer Games

"I'm Only Trying To Help You" (IOTTHY) is a co-dependent game that triggers a host of good and bad feelings for both the Helper and the person who gets rescued. It is a game because it goes beyond a natural human desire to give and receive help. Giving and receiving help without ulterior motivation can be a positive experience for both parties involved.

The "IOTTHY" game is motivated by neediness: the need to rescue others and feel noble, the need to persecute and feel superior or the need to overcome the hopeless, helpless feelings that go with the Victim role.

> The Rescuer suggests to her adult daughter, "You know, if you just kept a budget like Dad and I do, you wouldn't have such a time with your bills."
>
> Mom feels noble for being such a helping mother but daughter says, "Look, Ma, please. I'm getting by."
>
> In Mother's mind that sounds like "Bug off" which triggers a switch into her Persecutor role. She says, "You never would listen to reason."
>
> Daughter flashes anger, "There you go again. Treating me like a little girl."
>
> "Well, I'm only trying to help." Feeling hurt and unappreciated, Mother gathers her things to leave.
>
> Daughter snaps, "I don't need your help." She feels irritated and resentful. Later those feelings give way to guilt. A few days later they get together and play a game of "Kiss And Make Up," which opens up the next round of "IOTTHY."

When you are playing "IOTTHY" in a Persecutor role, doing what seems to be your duty can quickly invite the anger of others. Your righteousness gives way to anger when "Helpless" players ignore or reject the rules you feel they "should" obey.

If you try to play this game as a Victim, you know the feelings of having everything go wrong once again. What starts out to be a well-intentioned offer of help turns into a game of "Stupid" or "Kick Me" because it is inappropriate: The would-be Rescuer is either incompetent or doesn't see the reality that no one has asked for help.

If this game of "I'm Only Trying To Help You" is familiar and you want to get out of it, take a tip from Ann Landers. Time after time she advises her readers to "MYOB" (Mind Your Own Business). Following this advice has been difficult for me in the process of change. One family rule in our house made me my brother's keeper, and I liked the good strokes that came from doing that. It took many years and some bitter experiences to realize that my duty was to "live and let live." The more I do that now the better my life goes.

This is not to imply that all desire to help others should be suppressed or denied. There are legitimate times and ways to offer and receive help. The best I know is to simply ask, "Would you like some help?" If your offer is accepted, great. You can give of yourself and enjoy the feelings that come from it. If your offer is rejected, stop right there. Don't push your need to help onto the other person, no matter how much you might think they need it. To accept rejection without resentment means you are moving away from games and toward authenticity and greater autonomy in your relationships.

Other Co-dependent Games

There are many games of co-dependency. It isn't necessary to know them all, but it is useful to have at least a nodding acquaintance with the most popular ones. Here are four that are easy to spot once you've become familiar with the principles we've already discussed:

"Harried," sometimes called the Workaholism Game, is often played to satisfy the need to feel important or to

avoid intimacy. For hard-core players the hidden purpose is
to create ulcers, heart attacks or other illnesses. Doctors
now tell us that behavior such as this may account for as
much as 70 percent of the diseases suffered by people living
in the modern world.

"See What You Made Me Do" is a basic blame-game,
justifying anger at others in an attempt to cover up our
own character flaws or incompetency.

"See How Hard I Tried" is a game for avoiding blame or
responsibility. Those playing this game demand credit for
their effort despite their failures. (For many years I salved
the wounds of losing by telling myself, "Well, I really tried
hard." It was a reenactment of many childhood scenes when
Mother said the same in an effort to counteract the pain I
felt when my stepfather ridiculed me.)

"Uproar" is the inevitable result of "One Up/One Down"
transactions. The power person comes away with a false
sense of winning and the passive person is left with feelings
of resentment and helplessness. It is a game that substitutes
excitement for intimacy.

For example, when things don't go according to Jason's
expectations he demands explanations, his voice rises and
he jabs the air with his fist, just as his father did. When this
happens the Child in Janet is frightened. His aggressive
behavior triggers her passivity. Her mind literally blocks
and she is unable to give Jason the explanation he seeks.

Their game of "Uproar" usually ends up in an impasse.
Janet breaks into tears and runs into another room, just
as her mother did, or Jason storms out for a trip to the
neighborhood bar, just as his father did.

Recognizing the games you and others play increases your
awareness of what *really* goes on in your relationships. However, with that awareness comes a major decision about the way
you're going to spend your time.

The time you spend alone or with others, in social rituals,
pastimes, work and play can increasingly become a matter of
choice rather than habit or compulsion. You need no longer
slavishly follow the automatic responses dictated by the games
you learned in childhood. As you work out of these games you

will be delighted to find a vast new world out there, much bigger than the one in which your games have trapped you.

Some will not be willing to go along with you in your new way of being in the world. Fighting to maintain the status quo, they will test your new resolve to be an autonomous person instead of a partner in co-dependent games. Some will try desperately to "save you from yourself" and keep you as you are. Some will drift away. Don't blame them for their misdirected efforts. As gracefully and painlessly as you can, strive for your autonomy and let them make their own choices.

Internal Games

Your move toward autonomy will also affect the way you spend time with yourself. Your increasing awareness of game-playing will include noticing the games that go on within your head. Gradually you will become aware of your internal dialogue, with the Punitive Parent berating the Aggrieved Child, and the resulting childhood feelings of anxiety and inadequacy. You'll also come to see how the games we play inside our heads are the real source of the bad feelings we experience through the games we play with people.

What To Do Instead Of Playing Games

When people ask me what they can do instead of playing games, my first answer is to keep on with your self-education. You may come upon phrases or paragraphs that will motivate you with insights about the ways you relate to others. Many people find meditation both helpful and enjoyable. It can help you quiet the voices in your inner world and escape the bad feelings that accompany them. Others find the same pleasure and insight in physical exercise such as walking, cycling, swimming or jogging. Above all, break free of your games and learn to play. Nurture the Child in you who very likely never learned to play.

"Serenity" is the key to a game-free life and that comes only when we give up the "toxic excitement" of relationships dominated by games. Giving up toxic excitement is a difficult step along the way of recovery. Often this step is responsible for the "Is-this-all-there-is?" feeling that sometimes comes as we slowly learn to trade anxiety for enthusiasm, deepening intimacy and the subtle but deeply satisfying pleasure of serenity.

Wishing for serenity is one thing. Choosing it and making it happen is quite another. There are many who wish for serenity but do little to make it happen in their lives. They talk about it. They go to groups. They wonder why it doesn't come to them. And they are not to be blamed for that. Some lack skills and information needed for making change. Others came out of their dysfunctional family systems with such deep feelings of not being okay that they literally believe there is no hope for them. Not knowing that their destructive games can be surrendered in favor of choosing autonomy and intimacy, they despair that happiness will never come to them.

Whatever your co-dependency, be assured that your understanding of the dynamics of game-playing will immediately begin changing communication habits that have long had negative impacts on your relationships. Thousands of us have improved our family and work life by learning these new ways to communicate.

An Action Plan

Here are some actions you can take to help you break away from the games that echo dysfunctional communication habits that you learned in childhood.

1. Be on the alert for your "automatic" response to other people; these are old programs emerging.
2. Learn to recognize voice tones you employ as Persecutor or Victim and practice new ways of using your voice to sound more positive and receptive.
3. Avoid game-players whenever possible.
4. Spend your free time with people who are autonomous or growing out of game-playing.
5. Disengage yourself when you sense a game is coming on.
6. Don't look for other people to rescue you.
7. Don't allow yourself to be cast in the role of Victim.
8. Avoid criticizing others no matter how "justified" it may seem.
9. Give positive strokes to others as often as possible.

10. Accept whatever praise is offered with a simple "Thank you." Learn to bask in the sunshine of positive feedback.

11. Give up saying "You should" and "You ought to." Alternatives are "You might" or "Maybe this will work."

12. Practice active listening, giving people feedback on what you understand them to be saying. Phrases that can help you with this are: "I get the feeling you're (angry, sad, glad, etc.)." "Would you be willing to tell me more about that?" "How would you like me to respond to that?"

This is just a beginning list of the many actions you can take to avoid or extricate yourself from games. Once you catch on to the basic principles it will become increasingly easy for you to develop ways which seem natural to you. As you embark on this new venture remember something that is repeatedly said in recovery groups: "Take it easy!"

Don't sabotage your efforts by impulsively confronting others with the "new you." Much as you might want to heal the hurt connected with your past communication habits, go slowly. When one part of a system changes the whole system changes. Everyone involved in a system struggles to keep the familiar inner stability that was there before you changed. It is almost as though the system itself starts battling to maintain the status quo.

If you happen to be the co-dependent breaking out of the system, chances are you're going to be confronting a classic "double bind." The quesiton is, "How do I change my games, become the person I want to be, and not lose my partner, parent, child, boss or significant other?"

It is a paradoxical question because you are the only one who can provide the answer. You often become a positive model for others in your life, giving them a new way of looking at the world. When this happens others change without much effort from you except that of living an autonomous life. At the opposite extreme, relationships that were based on games and co-dependency sometimes end. While this may be painful, it also opens doors to a new way of life with others who are also looking for serenity and deeper intimacy in their relationships.

There are no guarantees when it comes to giving up games. Like everything else in life, the road to living by choice instead of habit has its up and downs. "Mistakes" are not failures as long as you recognize your setbacks as learning opportunities on your path to authenticity and a game-free life. You cannot assume that anyone, even those closest to you, will want to go along with the new you. How they deal with your changes is for them to decide. A major test of your recovery will be your willingness to let go of the need to control the destiny of others.

Keep in mind that the significant others in your relationships may be completely satisfied with you as you are and may not welcome change in your co-dependent status. Persecutors need Victims to persecute. Rescuers need Victims to rescue. And Victims need Victims with whom to share their misery. To stand apart from the enmeshments of co-dependency and be autonomous is not an easy task. But the effort to do so brings its own rewards and its own joys.

Risk and walk on, and the answers to your doubts and anxieties will come to you, often in ways you could not even imagine. As you feel your way along you will find what fits for you.

From my own experience I can assure you that one of the toughest struggles for autonomy comes from within, from our own Inner Saboteurs. There is a part of every co-dependent person that encourages us to sabotage our own efforts at finding a new way of being. Here's how my Inner Saboteur did this:

In my early enthusiasm for the writings of Eric Berne I impulsively tried to carry the message of transactional analysis to a whole bunch of people I knew who didn't want it. I suffered quite a few putdowns before it got through to me that I couldn't play my game of "I'm Only Trying To Help" with the whole world. And I imagine my games of "Transactional Analysis" led some of my recovering friends to decide I had failed to relinquish my arrogance and sense of self-importance.

If others in your "people system" (family, friends, spouses, peers or work group) agree to join you in your efforts at change, that is wonderful. However, be prepared if that cooperation isn't forthcoming. In the absence of mutually acceptable agreements your sudden change in communication style can result in their ending the relationship.

For example, a young executive of my acquaintance went off to a weekend seminar to find what the group called his "authentic self." The following Monday he returned to work and, in his words, "really leveled with my boss."

"For the first time in my life," he said, "I was honest. I told him I was sick and tired of playing his games, and said from now on everything had to be on the up and up."

I asked him, "So what happened?"

"He fired me. That's what happened."

The moral of the story is, "Go slow." Think things out in advance before you suddenly announce that you want everyone around you to change. You don't need to stop other people from playing games in order to enjoy your own autonomy. Just don't let yourself get "hooked." The bottom line is that there is only one person you need to change, and that is you.

Using your head to think things through and decide what is appropriate for you is the essence of autonomy and recovery from co-dependency. Every victory, large or small, earns you more self-granted permission to be yourself and interact with others in ways that you choose.

Caution Signs On The Road To Recovery

One word of warning as you go about mingling with others newly entered on the way to recovery. The games men and women play in their instincts for mating go on in recovery just as they do in all walks of life.

When sex gets into the act, the obsessive grip of old scripts is hard to escape. Old roles supplant authenticity. The games of rescuing can be confused with compassion; love and pity can get mixed up. Archaic family rules can be rekindled and have a negative influence on establishing new female/male relationships.

Don't, however, let your caution keep you away from ACoA or CoDA (co-dependency) self-help groups. These provide a wonderful way to increase your awareness of the games you and others play. On those days when your own emotional balance is relatively stable, practice your listening skills. Listen for tones of anger, guilt and self-pity, and contrast these to the clear, calm voices radiating self-confidence that come from those who are in charge of their lives.

Listen for the conflict revealed by vocal tones that don't seem to match the words and which leave you puzzled. Be aware of your impulses to respond as you might outside the group. Would your vocal tones, words and body language ordinarily trigger Rescuer or Persecutor responses? Does the sexual identity of a speaker make a difference in your feelings toward her or him?

Early in my work as a group leader I found that with certain women I had difficulty expressing myself as a calm, collected professional. After one workshop I realized that one assertive red-haired woman had triggered my habitual resistance to all symbols of authority. It was an example of what can happen when a professional has not yet resolved one of their own issues.

Mary Goulding helped me work this out while I was training in Redecision Therapy. She could hear my stress on the audio tapes I brought in for supervision. One day while I was working with her, she sensed my difficulty in dealing with a woman in the "expert's seat." Mary firmly said, "Joe, I am not your mother."

I looked at her blankly. I was mute and felt stupid, just as I had as a little kid confronted by any figure of authority.

Mary gently said, "What are you feeling, Joe?"

I said, "Nothing. Empty."

"How old are you?"

"Right now? About eight, I guess."

"You felt that way often?"

"Sure. Every time my mother or grandmother scolded me."

"Joe, what did your mother look like?"

I got a picture of her in my mind. "Tall. Square-shouldered. Kind of fierce sometimes."

Mary smiled. "Red-headed?"

"Sure." The group laughed and I laughed, too, relieved to know that I'd found another key to my habitual response to assertive women.

Of course, in an ACoA or CoDA group you don't have the help of a master therapist to assist you in your interactions with others. Nevertheless, by listening and learning in such groups, you can become aware of the old tapes in your memory bank and increasingly unhook yourself from habitual self-de-feating responses.

In your self-help groups keep in mind that, although it is appropriate to be alert to the behaviors of others, it is wise to keep your focus on you. As a co-dependent you've already spent too much time focusing on others. It's time to make you your Number One priority. It's time to consider the joy of living as game-free as you possibly can, enjoying the fruits of effective communications in all your relationships. It's time to enjoy serenity and intimacy in all your close connections.

Summing Up

All this talk of games and becoming game-free has one goal: to raise our awareness of what goes on in our relationships. The denial that for many years has protected us from real or imagined threats has also stood between us and the knowledge required to achieve emotional maturity. In *Healing The Child Within* Charles Whitfield writes, "Only an estimated 12 percent of our life and our knowledge is in our *conscious* awareness, in contrast to 88 percent that is in our *unconscious* awareness." (6)

If you have chosen the road of recovery, from this day forward your daily living, reading, involvement with support groups, therapy and healthier interactions with others will all contribute to your "conscious" awareness. Conscious awareness becomes a beacon in the darkness, chasing out the unconscious motives that might otherwise control your life. Using that increased awareness, putting it into action, is what personal growth is all about.

Whenever faced with difficult decisions, you might want to remind yourself once again that the answer to your life problems are not found in others, they are found in you.

❦ 4 ❧

Rowena's Story

The search for serenity begins with a willingness to discover and honestly recognize the areas in our own lives where we did not quite grow up.

— **Lewis F. Presnall**

"If *he'd* just change, everything would be okay." If you've ever thought that, you know what life is like for women whose childhood programming has left them with a dysfunctional, co-dependent script. Rowena grew up with such a script.

Long before the term "adult child of an alcoholic" came into common usage, Rowena knew she was one. She didn't know that someday she would read statements like, "Adult children tend to experience difficulty with trust, intimacy, control, perfectionism, guilt and low self-esteem."

Today she looks at a description like that, shrugs her shoulders and says, "That's sure the way it's been for me."

She also says, "It's too bad we didn't know about these things a lot sooner in life."

That's certainly true. Our lives are too full now for us to waste time "crying over spilt milk." Rowena hopes more older women will recognize that age need not be a barrier to recovery from co-dependency.

The Roots Of Rowena's Co-dependency

This excerpt from Rowena's journal reveals the shame that went with being the daughter of an alcoholic:

Reading the journal of Judy in *Lost In The Shuffle*, I recognized lots of similarities between her childhood and mine. I don't have the feelings and reactions now about what happened to me, as she said she had when writing about her childhood. Perhaps it's because I'm older and have had more time to flatten my emotions, more years to practice being invisible.

I can relate to the feelings of helplessness like I had whenever Dad was angry and physically abusing Mom or my brothers and to the feelings of relief and guilt about not being the one abused. Mom did try to protect us from him, but I'd always rather she didn't because it meant he'd let up on us kids and take out his anger on her twice as bad.

Although I had it a lot better than the boys did, I felt sorry for myself because I was all alone at night in my own room while Walter and George were together in theirs. Of course, they each wanted their own room and were envious of me. We always had a dog and I was allowed to have it in my room with me, yet I can never remember it being in the house at any time except bedtime so I'm sure Dad was trying to be kind to me.

Dad was always promising to take us kids on picnics or fishing or to the movies but usually he'd get loaded and then angry at us, Mom especially, because we couldn't leave at the exact moment he decided he was ready to go. Or else when we'd go to a show or to a cafe (rarely and usually if we were traveling), he'd stagger or call attention to us in some way so I always thought people were laughing at us. I just hated going any place with him.

I loved going on picnics with Mom and the boys because we always had a good time. The boys would go off down the creek by themselves and I'd have Mom alone and we'd look for wild flowers and funny bugs.

I followed Mom around like a good little girl because she was nice to me and protected me from Dad's ranting and raving. My first memory of her letting me down, just like Dad, when she promised me she'd do something and then didn't, was when I was five. She told me she'd go to Sunday School with me on a certain Sunday so I could be baptized. She sewed me a pretty white dress with pink ribbons and a big pink bow and bought me a pair of black patent leather slippers. I was looking forward to going down the church aisle with her.

I got all dressed up and Mom was dressing when Dad came in. He'd had a big fight with a customer. He accused Mom of wanting to go to church so she could screw the preacher and ripped her dress off her. She told me she was sorry she couldn't go with me as she'd promised but told me to go on by myself. I knew she had to stay home to calm Dad down, but I was hurt. I think I hated Dad for sure that day.

I had gone to Sunday School many times by myself but never to be baptized. I went to the church and sat in the back row and watched others kids go down the aisle with their parents. I was too afraid to go by myself so I sat still. The preacher's wife spoke up and said there was one more little girl to be baptized, and she came back and took me down the aisle. I felt so proud because I was the only person the preacher's wife led to the altar, although I still felt sorry Mom wasn't there.

Arguments, rage, physical violence and hallucinatory episodes were a constant in Rowena's childhood. Yet, from the time at age six that she had to take Daddy's dinner to him in the one-cell, stone jailhouse on the outskirts of town, until age 13 when he had to be taken to the county hospital, she never heard the word "alcoholic." His drinking was never discussed with the kids around. It's doubtful that Rowena's mother ever confronted her with her husband's drinking. Even after he'd seen giant grasshoppers coming through the wall and had to be taken away, he wouldn't tolerate any thought of being classified as alcoholic. He threatened to sue the doctor who dared to enter "chronic alcoholic" in his medical record.

Rowena's strategy for survival in the midst of all this turmoil was to stay away from everybody and be as invisible as possible. She felt she'd be safe if she just didn't do anything. She also learned that if she didn't make any decisions but just went along with what life brought her, there were always kindly neighbors, teachers, preachers' wives and other Rescuers who would solve her problems for her. Early in life she decided that "going along" was the safest way to "get along."

Another entry in her journal demonstrates how childhood beliefs and behaviors bind a co-dependent to constant reenactment in the present of reactions learned in the past. Until very recent years Rowena had been plagued by an inability to stay focused when the circumstances of the moment triggered old tapes that reminded her of some traumatic childhood experience. At such times she simply "tripped out," ran away in her mind and avoided dealing with the situation at hand. This is how she writes of such "triggers" and reactions in her journal:

Times when I've had the "get away from it" feelings

1. Whenever Dad was drunk and abusing Mom or my brothers.

2. Whenever he was drunk and wanted to kiss me and he smelled of sour wine.
3. When he threw my report card on the floor. He asked, "How many loaves of bread will that buy?" (His sister and three brothers had gone to the University of California but a reversal of family finances had only provided him a chance to go to mechanics school. He put down everyone who stood above him in the pecking order as he perceived it.)
4. Whenever Joe and I had arguments — when we had both been drinking.
5. Whenever Joe and someone else were having a discussion that sounded like an argument to me.

Distressful feelings in the here and now feel the same for many of us as they did in childhood, even though there's been a change of age and circumstances. Some call these "carried feelings."

The most familiar of Rowena's "carried feelings" was cold fear, something like a freezing hand that gripped her stomach from the inside out. She felt as though she wanted to run away but was frozen in place. For years she'd wake up nights with that same feeling. She couldn't say what was in her dreams, but she could feel the feeling almost as though some frosty ghost had visited her in the night.

Post-Traumatic Stress Reactions

When Rowena is suddenly stricken by these flashes of memories from her stressful past, her mind goes blank. She "rubber bands" and her frightened familiar feelings of the past snap back and overwhelm her thinking process in the present. (1) As a little girl she couldn't get her feelings into words. The intense conflict between fear and the desire to scream out against the tyranny of her father's alcoholic behavior shut down her mind and froze her feeling system. She suffered "psychic numbing" which as Cermak says, provided her with an "illusion of safety and control." He speaks of this condition as a "survival mode" that allows the world to just wash by. (2)

In the language of transactional analysis this condition is known as "contamination." The conflict in the mind between the Parent and the Child rages so the Adult ability to solve problems and make decisions is temporarily blocked by the resurrection of old thinking/feeling habits. As new, more appropriate thinking/feeling habits are developed, this numbing process can be alleviated or avoided in most cases.

There are still times when it is difficult for Rowena to put her feelings into words. If feeling pressured, she sometimes swoops her hands up like a little girl who is trying to describe her emotions. Of that she says, "I don't know. Just like when there's an argument, my head goes all swoosh inside. Everything blots out. I feel I've got to get away. I know there's nothing to be afraid of but I just want to be someplace else."

And get away she does, just as she did when she was a child. She disappears. The rest of our family is a very vocal group. What we consider discussions sound like angry arguments to her, the kind she endured in childhood. When that happens someone inevitably says, "Hey. Mom's gone again." She retreats to another room or the backyard, protected by the trees and flowers or Samantha, the basset hound.

Almost immediately after Rowena wrote in her journal about the fright her father's rages caused her, her ability to assert herself improved and the angry feelings that sometimes cloaked her fears began to subside. Identifying with another woman's story about co-dependency gave Rowena helpful new information and insights. Writing out her own story seemed to purge her of much unfinished business that needed closure.

Perhaps the best way to share Rowena's experience is in her own words from the following interview done by a friend.

Rowena's Recovery

Q. *When did you first feel your co-dependency was a problem for you?*

A. Well, I guess in a way it's always been a problem. But it didn't really bother me so much as a kid. I felt sorry for myself lots of times, especially when I was around the kids who had normal families and better clothes.

But I was healthy, played a lot. I never felt really okay around adults or anyone I thought was better than I was. I just kept quiet then.

Q. *That doesn't sound like your dad's alcoholism bothered you too much.*

A. Oh, no. I don't mean that. What else is there for a little kid to do except be who she is? I couldn't do anything about Dad's drinking. I felt sorry for myself a lot, felt sad a lot. Dad's drinking kept us broke. I was in the eighth grade before I got my first "store-bought" dress.

About that age was when I first really felt different because
the other kids had better clothes and things. I really felt "not-
okay" about that. But I used to get hand-me-downs from the
lady next door. And my high school sewing teacher gave me
dresses. I guess they felt sorry for me.

But I kind of liked that. Guess that was a part of my early co-
dependency, having someone be a rescuer and give me a helping
hand. It made me feel like I mattered to someone.

Q. *Did you have to be a people-pleaser to get along?*

A. You bet. I was a real people-pleaser. Kept quiet and smiled
a lot. Always minded Mother. But you know, in school I talked
a lot more. I got real good at playing "Poor Little Me." I'd tell my
friends' parents and my teachers how sad I was. Guess you
could call manipulating people a sign of co-dependency.

Q. *You told us how things were with your dad. How about your mother?*

A. Things were different with her. She didn't do much except
work and try to keep the peace. Took us away to relatives in
Michigan a couple of times. We didn't know why then. We
realized later it must have been during Dad's spells when he
was going into DTs or "getting religion." He didn't drag us to
church but he'd mutter a lot and talk about God and Jesus. One
time he put a big soup bone on a box in the cellar and prayed to
it while he was making his home brew.

I guess Mom was just a helpless co-dependent who couldn't
break away. She'd leave him but always go back until finally she
divorced him after us kids were grown. That's probably why
she didn't leave. Because of us. In my teens I'd get terribly angry
at her for not leaving but I just didn't understand what it was
like to be a poor, uneducated woman. He kept us fed, despite all
the booze. It wasn't 'til I was in social work, in my 40s, that I
understood how hard it is for women who get trapped like that.
Their existence and survival depend on a man.

Q. *You said something about manipulating people as a sign of co-
dependency. Can you tell us more about that?*

A. When I was a kid I couldn't get what I wanted by asking
for it straight out. So I pretended a lot, did my people-pleasing
stuff. Took care of my little brother so Mother wouldn't have
to. That made me a good girl. When I got older, I got away with
a lot by pretending to be a good girl.

Q. *Did you do that as an adult?*

A. Why not? If you're a passive co-dependent, what else are
you going to do when you want things your way? Lots of times

I didn't feel good about that but I guess that was what I thought was normal. It's awfully hard for me to level with people and say what I really feel, especially with Joe. It was just so scary to talk back to Dad. One time I did and he slapped me so I never tried again.

Q. *You just accepted your co-dependency?*

A. I guess I learned to live with it. But, look, I wasn't all that different from other people, especially women. You know in those days it was a *man's* world. Mom was in her 40s before she even got to vote.

But about accepting co-dependency, I guess so, but it wasn't really so bad. Like I said, I didn't figure I was that much different from other kids except they had better clothes and things.

Q. *You mean at times the co-dependency was worse than others?*

A. Well, you know what life is like for a kid. Most of the time you could say I was mainly a moderate co-dependent. I was what's called the Lost One. I was the same after I grew up. Most of the time I just took what came my way. Then there were some times when things were really bad for me, when I felt desperate or really depressed.

Q. *What made the difference?*

A. Different situations, I guess. Joe and I married in college. The co-dependency wasn't any problem then. He talked and I listened. I liked that. It took the heat off me when we were around other people.

We were two poor kids at a rich school and it was kind of us against them, the poor against the rich. We were broke but we had fun. There was a lot of excitement. I drank, too, in those days, so we partied a lot. Not like the other college kids. Five dollars would pay for an evening at the Biltmore or the Coconut Grove but we didn't have the money or the clothes for those places. So we wandered around a lot on Main Street in downtown Los Angeles, just a block off Skid Row. Two dollars there would buy 15 or 16 drinks and we could dance for free.

Q. *What changed?*

A. Hell, we had to grow up. The excitement went on for quite a while on the Mexican border when Joe was in the Border Patrol. Then we spent five years in Venezuela. But you know, romance and adventure got all bogged down by the time the third kid came along. By that time I was probably more than moderately co-dependent. Joe was still adventuring and I resented it. I felt left out.

Q. *Would you call that situational co-dependency?*

A. I guess so. But it didn't really get bad for me 'til later. All told there were three times when it seemed I'd lost all control of my life and was helpless to do anything about it. Life would go along okay and then situations would change and I'd hit bottom again.

Once the kids were in school, it seemed like I wasn't worth a damn. "Women's work" didn't cut it for me. Dad always said, "Women are only good for one thing." I believed I had to earn money to be worthwhile.

Q. *What did you do about that?*

A. At first I didn't do anything. I mean that literally. I just sat around the house and stared at the walls. I guess I scared Joe. One of his Kiwanis friends had a children's store so Joe helped me get a part-time job. Then I did volunteer work at the state hospital and that helped me get my mind off myself.

Q. *Did the volunteer work do anything for you?*

A. Absolutely. It helped me realize my life wasn't really all that bad. I feel a little ashamed admitting it, but I guess it made me feel better than some people. But mainly, volunteering gets you thinking about someone else's problems. That's what 12-Step work is all about, isn't it? Helping yourself by helping others.

Q. *So work was the answer for you?*

A. Not completely. It was for a while but if you've got a Victim script you'll find a way to make yourself unhappy. Joe was having some anxiety about his career. He began thinking about a job in Louisiana and I began worrying myself to death before he even put in an application for it.

I didn't want any more of the oil business. I'd had enough of that macho stuff in South America. I didn't want to live in the South. I'd taken a job as a social worker and was beginning to feel like somebody. But I couldn't tell him I didn't want to move so I just buried my fear inside me until it showed up in my body. I ate to compensate. I had trouble swallowing. My arms got so heavy, I couldn't do my paperwork.

Q. *Your co-dependency immobilized you?*

A. Almost, I guess, but I didn't see it that way. It wasn't like now. Ordinary people didn't know all this psychological language they use now. Sometimes I thought I was going crazy but the doctor said there was nothing wrong with me.

Q. *Is that all?*

A. No. He gave me some diet pills that got me all charged up. I lost some weight. I felt better about that. Got caught up in my work. Had a lot of artificial energy. I guess the pills gave me some courage. I worked up the nerve to tell Joe I didn't want to move.

Q. *How did that go over with him?*

A. That's the funny thing. He changed careers and went into selling so we wouldn't have to move. That was the first time in 17 years of marriage I got something important to me just by asking for it.

Q. *Was that a breakthrough for you?*

A. In a way, I guess, but it didn't change all my co-dependency. The pills got me so charged up, I couldn't sleep and my brain ran so fast, I couldn't make my thoughts come out straight. So I quit the pills. Thank goodness. People didn't know then how addictive diet pills can be.

Anyway, I felt better. With the fear of moving away out of my mind, I got better at my work. But you know, in my childhood the message was, "Life's a struggle." Happiness wasn't on the menu. I figured some day I'd die and go to heaven so I struggled along pretty good 'til I thought Joe's drinking would do him in like it did my dad.

Q. *How did you handle that?*

A. Not too good. They didn't do interventions then. Besides, I couldn't do that. No one could ever say anything about my dad's drinking. I was the same way with Joe. And my friends in Al-Anon all said I just had to wait 'til he hit bottom.

Then when he did quit drinking, the situation improved and I was okay again. I don't mean okay in the way it might have been if I'd become a more self-dependent person. But as long as I worked I felt worthwhile. Then when the kids were all gone, I began doing some things with Joe and took a little TA training. It was fun going to conferences and seminars.

Q. *What happened after you retired?*

A. I hit the skids again. Went into a big depression. All the old tapes about worthlessness began playing again. I just couldn't accept the fact that raising a family and having a career for 20 years gave me enough credit to feel good about myself. Still couldn't accept anything good about me.

We moved over to the coast. I thought being out of the heat and near the ocean would help. It didn't. Then Lynn, our youngest daughter, asked me to go with her to apply for a waitressing job at the Roaring Camp Recreational Park.

I only wanted to help her, do some more rescuing, but they offered me a job so I spent two years waiting tables at the barbecue pits. I loved that, meeting all the tourists from all over the world. Besides it put some money in my purse that never got into our joint account. It gave me back some independence. But about age 65, handling the trays and the clean-up work got too much for me.

Q. *You seem pretty happy now. What happened?*

A. Oh, that's hard to answer. Aging, maybe. I know time doesn't heal all wounds but I guess I accepted the fact that my body didn't want to work anymore so I might as well be satisfied with what peace of mind I had.

Q. *You mean you finally just outgrew your co-dependency?*

A. No, I wouldn't say that. For one thing, don't think I think I'm cured. I've still got a lot of old tapes that bug me. I still have feelings that bother me. But I know a lot more now about what to do when I feel depressed or angry. I'm pretty happy now. At last.

Q. *How did that happen?*

A. Oh, that's tough. I don't know. By osmosis from Joe and Lynn, I guess. No, I'm putting myself down again. A bunch of things happened but it's hard to make any kind of logical order out of them. Joe was into doing some classes on retirement planning and he pushed at me about my painting. Then a neighbor invited me to go to her art class. Now I go to classes two days a week and do a lot of painting on my own. When I paint, I get lost in that so there's no time left to hassle myself with all that "Not okay" junk.

Q. *You mean having a hobby helps with your co-dependency?*

A. Sure, why not? But maybe what I mean is it helps ease some of the built-in stress. Then, too, our daughter Lynn got turned on to the ACoA thing and that got Joe thinking about it. The co-dependency stuff came after that.

He and Lynn talked about it a lot and I listened. She and Whitney, the oldest girl, asked me a lot of questions about my childhood and that got me thinking some. I read some of their books. I already knew enough about life scripts and my games to use what I knew about TA. I gave up letting the Parent voices in my head beat on my Child all the time for not being good enough. Maybe it's like making bread pudding. You get a lot of stuff in the pot and stir it up and then it comes out okay.

Q. *What's worked best for you?*

A. Several things. Joe dragged me off to some ACoA groups and then some CoDA groups. I'm just not a self-starter. When I was a little girl it didn't seem like anything I'd do would ever come true, so why start anyway? I know in my head that the right groups are good places for learning. It's just that in the Child part of me, I'm so afraid people will laugh at me, so I'm on guard all the time. But nobody did laugh at me at the meetings. That was a good experience. Just being myself. I learned a lot by listening. Books help me a lot. I can read something and then go back and read it again 'til I get it. I use the CoDA affirmations a lot. And the Serenity Prayer.

Q. *Did you just go to groups to please Joe?*

A. Not completely. I went to some groups with him in his early abstinence. Then I went to quite a few TA groups with him about five years later. We learned a lot about communicating better. Partly I liked doing things together and partly I figured I was helping him. You know, the Rescuer thing. But I did do some co-leading with him.

I guess you could say I did it more for him than for me. That was my form of denial. I figured he was the one with the problems. But I admit a lot of it did rub off on me. Anyway, I'm not saying, "Do what I did." You can do better than that. You have more information available than I did. Now I can connect my TA stuff with my co-dependency and figure some things out for myself. One thing I do know for sure is that I hope others get started on recovery sooner than I did.

Q. *What's been the hardest issue for you to deal with?*

A. Self-pity. Anger first, maybe, and then the self-pity when my anger wouldn't get me what I wanted. I don't mean getting material things. I mean feeling good about myself, like feeling "equal to" instead of "less than."

Q. *What made life different for you when you learned about co-dependency?*

A. The biggest thing is accepting myself as I am. Just being okay with me. Feeling in my heart I am a good person, not feeling I have to be perfect and giving up the self-pity. Besides, we're both past 70. Age has to mellow you some. Joe's decided he's got all he can do just running his own life so he doesn't push me like he used to. I feel like I have more options now than I used to. I don't have to follow my old habits.

Q. *That sounds like Joe changed. What did you do to change?*

A. I do a lot of work in my journal. Digging up a lot of things from the past and getting them out of my system. It's work and sometimes it hurts, but writing things out seems to work for me. With my affirmations I guess I reprogram my thinking about myself.

With all the exposure to TA and games and all that, it's still hard for me to remember what I'm doing when I get myself into games. It used to be awfully hard for me to think in terms of "I'm OK — You're OK." I always thought everyone else was okay but not me. The more comfortable I get with myself, the easier it is to keep out of the stupid games and avoid all the silly fighting we used to do.

Like I said, the journal writing does a lot for me, especially because it's still hard for me to open up in a group. But in the end it's up to you to find out what works for you.

Q. *Lots of people get scared in groups. Can you tell me more about your fears?*

A. Well, for me it's just the same as it was as a kid. I was always afraid I'd be ridiculed, that someone would call me stupid or that I'd cry. I still am afraid I'll say the wrong thing or not say what I "ought to."

Q. *But you look so happy and contented. Did you always look like that?*

A. Not always maybe, but most of the time. After all, that's part of being "a good little girl." I was always supposed to hide my anger or my sadness. It's just been the last few years I've been able to be assertive instead of angry or ask Joe to hold me when I'm sad. That's hard for me but it gives me good feelings to be able to do it.

Q. *If you were doing your life again what would you do differently?*

A. I'd do what you're doing right now. I'd get all the information I could that would help me understand my co-dependency so I could change. If you can afford it, even if you have to make some sacrifices, find a good therapist and work through your childhood programming. I guess some of you call that family-of-origin issues. Learn to feel your feelings, learn you're worthwhile and you have the right to be yourself.

Q. *Would you get out of a bad marriage if you were in one?*

A. That depends on what you call bad. If you mean physical abuse, yes. If you mean emotional abuse, then I'd have to know more about that. It took me a long time to see that I was one of the players in the games we played. I was just as responsible as Joe. I acted out passive while he acted out aggressive. I don't mean physically. It's just that he survived by being a pusher and I survived by being a 'pushee.'

Q. *You've passed your Golden Wedding anniversary. Didn't you ever want to divorce him?*

A. Oh, sure. When I was mad. But then I'd get over the anger. Remember, I have an old-fashioned life script. In my script women are supposed to stay married and stick by their men. Divorce is failure and failure is hard for me to take.

Maybe one reason we stayed together so long is we both had a lot of abandonment as kids. One psychologist said we stayed together for all the wrong reasons but it seemed to work for us. A lot of our compatibility was based on our mutual co-dependency.

One of you said something about situational co-dependency. Seems like that applies to both of us because when the world is going right, we get along just great. Unless one of us gets hungry for negative strokes, we keep out of game-playing and all that garbage. Especially the self-pity stuff.

Q. *What do you mean you get hungry for negative strokes?*

A. That's part of the script. If I fall into my Victim role, I do stupid things and invite negative strokes. Most of the attention I got from my dad was negative so I guess I got in the habit. When I get positive strokes they just go right on by me. I used to think Joe was only trying to flatter me when he said something good. I'd feel manipulated. I wouldn't believe anything good about myself.

If Joe's feeling okay, he ignores all this negative stuff. If he's not, we get into the "fussies." When there're two co-dependents recovering at the same time, it takes some doing to keep on the right track with each other.

Q. *What do you do now about your low self-esteem?*

A. I try to put it aside. Keep at my positive affirmations. Remind myself I'm okay just as I am. Turn off the Parent voice that says I'm no damn good and get on with something else.

Sometimes I just sit on the couch and stare through the window at the hills and poppies and think about nature. Only I don't think so much. I just sit and look and that's peaceful.

Q. *You're in your 70s and you're still working at recovery?*

A. Well, I wouldn't call it working so much anymore. I don't have to fight the pain I used to suffer. The old tapes are still there but they don't pop up so often. And Joe's a lot more accepting now so I don't feel so pushed and resentful. It's bad enough having me pick at myself without having him doing it, too. But we've both made a lot of changes. Knowing about life scripts and our family-of-origin stuff has helped us mellow out a lot. It helped a lot with our kids, too.

Q. *You think all the work is worth it?*

A. You bet. Better late than never. Being a happy survivor beats just hanging on to survival like I used to. I feel like I'm me now more than I've ever felt before.

I wish I'd made more changes sooner but there's no point in hassling myself about that now. I wish I'd had the guts for more feeling therapy but I didn't hang in there the way I should have. You've got a lot more chances for help than I had. Whatever you do, go to some ACoA or CoDA meetings. They helped me a lot, made me realize my life wasn't all that bad and lots of people have a lot more problems than I ever had. I can't feel very sorry for myself when I know there are others in worse shape.

So go to meetings. Educate yourself about recovery. The most important thing I can say to you is find out what makes sense to you or feels right for you. If you're unhappy and you're willing to change, you'll find a way.

A Note About Personal Histories

If you are in recovery and are a parent, sharing your personal history with your children can be a wonderful, healing experience for all of you. Don't push it on them if they don't want it. Just let them know you are willing and available if they want to hear it.

Rowena and I must have talked about this chapter for at least six months before we got it on paper. We stirred up a lot of buried memories. And some of the little secrets married people often hold back from each other came up. We gained some new understandings of things that had been puzzling us in the past because we weren't forthright with each other.

We invited two of our children, Whitney and Lynn, to edit this chapter and talk about their memories of childhood. Going over the past in this way helped us with our memories and it helped them, too; we were all able to ask questions about the old family rules and the dysfunction we shared. Our children got a big kick out of learning things they'd never known about Rowena.

The sharing of our personal histories with our kids has been an important step in our recovery and theirs. It might be the same for you. Be careful though, if you do share, that you are in a good place with yourself and can handle the many kinds of feelings that can come up when a co-dependent family comes together in a time of intimacy. In our case, sharing our histories gave all of us a sense of having roots and nourished our growth as a family.

❧5❧

Growing In Groups

Man was "made" for fellowship, i.e., he is a social being; and when he violates his human connectedness, he dies.

— O. Hobart Mowrer

Most of life is a group experience. How we connect with our families, co-workers and communities largely determines the quality of our existence. As human connectedness improves, so does our overall well-being.

Healthy communication skills can only be learned with the "hands on" experience of interacting with other human beings.

Compatibility — "the ability to exist together in harmony" — is difficult for co-dependents. Skills in "give and take" simply weren't provided in our families of origin. Unfortunately, our parents and teachers defined compatibility as compliance with their wishes. We never learned the kind of "equal to" dynamics required for true compatibility.

The dynamics of human interaction we did learn were the three "F's": fight, flight, or freeze. We continue those habitual patterns in adulthood by:

1. Fighting back in anger.
2. Taking flight in passive compliance.
3. Freezing and splitting off from our feelings.

We continue these reactions until we painfully discover that the old ways aren't working for us any more. When that time came for me, I didn't know which way to turn. I felt I'd done all I could do about changing myself, mostly through Alcoholics Anonymous (AA). In those days psychotherapy was considered a No-No for recovering alcoholics, at least in my area. There were no ACoA or Co-dependents Anonymous groups to turn to. Looking for something I couldn't define and not knowing how to get it, I found myself in a crowd of others who were groping for their answers to life through involvement in groups, communes or cults.

Groping And Grouping

Without a label like co-dependency to identify my psychological discomfort, I joined thousands of others caught up in the human potential movement of the late 1960s. We sought identity, community and enlightenment, each of us defining those words in our own way.

Looking back now I'd say all of us, except for a few out-and-out crazies, were struggling with various issues of co-dependency. We were all searching for our own voices rather than going on as little more than an echo of our childhood programming. We'd grown tired of the wishful thinking that salvation comes from without rather than within.

As you search now for some new way along your own road of recovery, the odds are great that at some point you will want or need to explore the group experience for yourself. You will be presented with choices whether you ask for them or not. Friends will tell you with great enthusiasm about their favorite guru and urge you to go to a workshop or seminar with him. If you order a recovery book or go to a workshop, your name will soon be recorded on computerized mailing lists. In your mailbox you'll find a wide variety of flyers offering promises of a new and brighter life if you will just attend a certain lecture, seminar or workshop.

In the catalog of your local community college you may find classes listed under "Self Development" or "Personal Growth" that are meant for adult children of alcoholics or co-dependents. Many of these classes are conducted by local therapists and counselors. Attending such classes is a wise way of judging whether a particular professional might seem right for you if you consider individual therapy.

Millions of people have moved along their way toward autonomy in any of a multitude of time-tested ways. Some of the better-known ones are psychocybernetics, reality therapy, behavior modification, Gestalt therapy, transactional analysis, human effectiveness and redecision therapy.

Selecting the group or groups best suited to your temperament and degree of co-dependency may be the first test of your willingness to get moving toward self-dependency. It is part of your responsibility for your future.

12-Step Groups

I hope you have already chosen to attend a 12-Step group for adult children of alcoholics or co-dependents. If not, by all means go to at least a few meetings and learn how some others experience their co-dependency and the 12-Step way of recovery. If that doesn't seem the right way for you, keep looking.

The way that works for you is the way for you. Choice-making is the foundation of autonomy and appropriate choices. We learn to make choices only by choosing, and that's an ongoing process of living and learning by our experience.

Some people find the answer to all their recovery needs in a 12-Step group. Some do not. The only way you'll ever find what works for you is through experiencing how your life gets better as you exercise the courage to change.

One fear you can set aside as you think about attending such a group is that of speaking out in public. Whether you speak up at your first meeting or any other meeting is up to you. No one is required to talk. If you do talk you are protected from challenge and judgmental opinion by the 'no-crosstalk rule.'

Three tangible benefits are immediately available to you by attendance at 12-Step meetings:

1. Identification

To identify with the history of a speaker or the stories of others at a CoDA meeting is to recognize that, as John Donne put it, "No man is an island, entire of itself." Identifying with other co-dependents can rescue us from the gloom of alienation and open our way to connecting with others joined in the common cause of recovery. Having a name for what disturbs them helps many people say, "Well, now I know what's wrong with me, I can start to work on it."

2. Information

Co-dependency as a trait, a characteristic or a personality disorder doesn't have a universally accepted definition. Until we are told we have it, we don't know exactly what's wrong with us any more than a child knows he has measles until somebody points at those strange blotches on his body and says, "That's measles."

One way you know if you've "got" co-dependency is by getting information from others who have identified themselves as co-dependents. Each person in a group may have a different way of dealing with their condition, but take what they say as useful information. After that you can choose for yourself what you believe will work for you.

3. Inclusion

The walls of isolation are built of bricks labeled "Don't speak," "Don't trust" and "Don't feel." Many of us move through life armored by these injunctions that separate us from friendship, support or a sense of community. We exclude ourselves from the friendship and compassion of others through our feelings of worthlessness. We distance ourselves from others by feeling we have to solve our problems on our own.

It takes courage to remove our character armor and run the risk of attracting love or the more terrible risk of rejection. To suddenly feel included is a powerful emotional experience, especially for those of us who have spent years believing we were on the outside looking in because of our own "Don't belong" injunctions.

To come out from behind those toxic barriers and feel a sense of inclusion in the fellowship of humanity can provide the motivation for learning new ways of interacting with others. "I am not alone" can be said a thousand ways, and all of them have been said at one time or another by someone attending their first 12-Step meeting.

Self-observation In A 12-Step Group

If you find comfort in a 12-Step meeting, there is no better place to begin the healing practice of self-observation. As you listen to others speak, pay attention to your own thoughts and feelings. What irritates you? What turns you on? What sounds workable? What do you reject even before you evaluate it?

Do you find yourself jumping to conclusions about people because of their appearance or what they say? Do you hesitate to speak because you fear you will deprive someone else of their chance or because you are afraid to say what is on your mind?

Be aware of the interactions going on about you. Such awareness can provide you with some guidelines for improving your own interactions with others, both in and out of meetings.

Listen carefully to those in the group who specifically state how they changed their attitudes and actions in the process of recovery. Pay attention to the methods they use to solve their life problems. Listen for what seems right for you to practice in your new way of being in the world.

Support

In 12-Step groups, sponsoring others is considered important to individual recovery, both for the sponsor and the new member. When you attend such a group, you will learn about sponsorship and how to find help in grasping the program. Sponsors help the inexperienced "learn the ropes" as they tackle the tasks of recovery.

Some groups make available a list of members who are willing to talk with others. Though specific "how to's" are not discussed in meetings, there are many members who will be glad to tell you how they solved certain problems. Help is usually only a phone call away.

However, with all this in favor of 12-Step groups, if such groups don't seem right for you, don't feel there is something wrong with you. There are a thousand and one reasons why some people latch onto the 12-Step lifestyle and some don't. There are also those who get some of what they need in a 12-Step group but supplement their recovery by such options as:

1. Therapy groups.

2. Life-skills training groups or classes conducted by train-
   ers or instructors, rather than by a therapist.
3. Marriage encounter groups, parent effectiveness training
   groups or a variety of support groups.

Self-Loyalty And Groups

Doubt, concern and worry about being on the right track are
quite common among all of us moving in the direction of self-
improvement. Whatever you do in your search for the best
group or groups for you, don't let yourself be unduly swayed by
inappropriate feelings of loyalty to one group or another. Don't
let a false sense of loyalty keep you from exploring group therapy, life skills training groups or whatever group experience
you feel might best meet your needs.

Extreme loyalty can be a symptom of co-dependency. Writing
about adult children of alcoholics, Janet Woititz says, " . . . so-
called 'loyalty' is more the result of fear and insecurity than
anything else." (1) Don't confuse gratitude with unreasonable
loyalty. Your first loyalty is to yourself.

And don't confuse self-loyalty with selfishness. Think of it as
what William Shakespeare meant when he wrote, "This above
all, to thine own self be true."

The Group Way Of Self-Discovery

The way of self-discovery is unpredictable. Logic may point us
in one direction but circumstances push us in another. Our needs
change as we move on to higher levels of consciousness. We learn
by learning. We grow by growing. We change by changing.

Gathering in groups we learn as others learn, grow as others
grow and change as others change. We are encouraged by the
success of others. When we make mistakes, our resolve is bol-
stered by the nurturing of others.

In group we begin as voyeurs, observing the process of
change at work with others. Then we try things on for size.
We risk, first in the group and then in the world. If our experience doesn't work in the world, we go back to group to fix
it. We use group wisdom to help us decide the appropriateness
of our new directions.

More than anything else in group, we make discoveries —
some minor, some major, some distressful, some painful. But
some are joyful, and it is the joy that keeps us going. Sometimes we discover we are doing a few things the "right" way,
a way appropriate to our growth, and with that experience
comes the good feeling of being true to ourselves and our own
individual journey.

Early in my group exploration, I made three unpleasant and
unwelcome but healthy discoveries I would not have made
otherwise. Hurtful though they were, those discoveries
opened the way for me to get on with the exciting challenge of
personal growth:

1. I discovered I was not the person I had imagined myself to
be. Mirrored by others, I slowly and painfully came to see I was
more a product of my imagination than of reality. The grandiosity
that unknowingly served as my protection against my low self-
esteem had twisted my vision of myself. Somewhere along the
way, I had lost the ability to see myself as I was seen by others.

2. While blindfolded and being led by a stranger on a "trust
walk" along a mountain path, I realized how little trust I put in
anyone to help me in any way. In childhood my trust in others
had been betrayed many times; my early life had been an un-
broken series of double binds.

I wanted so much to be accepted by others but I was always
the new kid in the boarding home or the new kid in school.
Somebody was always setting me up as the butt of their jokes
and I felt I had to be a good sport.

I grew up in the grip of a people-pleaser's paradox: I tried
hard to please my parents and peers, but I was always afraid I'd
be rejected. Somewhere along the line, my childhood decision
became "I can't trust anyone but myself." That's a lonely position
to be in. It cut me off many times from assistance I tried hard
to get — but sabotaged with my distrust of others.

Out of my group experience I've come to realize that the
more I trust myself, the easier it is to trust others. I've also
picked up a few mentors along the way who help me work
through my distrust when my mild but persistent fears of
betrayal are inappropriate.

3. My machismo bulwark of avoiding any kind of help from
others was so strong I couldn't break out of it by myself. It took
the manipulations of a skilled psychodrama director to bring
me to the point where "the walls came tumbling down." Without

that caring intervention I might have gone on forever without knowing the joy of decent self-regard and the richness of my relationship with Rowena in our golden years.

Psychodrama

The psychodrama environment is somewhat similar to a theater with a stage, a director, a star, a supporting cast and an audience. Under the supervision of the therapist/director the star acts out a problem, the cast interacts with the star and the audience provides pertinent feedback. Everyone concerned is exposed to new insights into human behavior and explores new ways of interacting with others. Participants in psychodrama may try out new roles for themselves and experience the thoughts and feelings that go with being the person they want to be in life.

In my case, the first crack in the protective walls of my psychic fortress came at the University of Utah Summer School Of Alcohol Studies. In my illusions of invincibility I volunteered for some role-playing in a psychodrama group that was demonstrating the Top Dog/Underdog nature of many marriages.

Without expecting it, I ended up in a confrontation with the Persecutor part of me. While playing a domineering husband, I got so deep into the role, I couldn't get out until the psychodrama director kindly called down the curtain.

I'd spent years faking it as Top Dog to protect myself from the feelings of the Underdog and the emotional habits of my childhood. In adult I "stuffed down" all feelings of being "less than" under an illusion that I was acting like a *man.* My "I'm OK — they're not OK" position deafened me to all words of criticism.

Experiencing the psychodrama situation and its emotional turmoil painfully introduced me to the first awareness that my self was something more than my conscious image of me. Not knowing what was going on with me, I spontaneously acted out my Top Dog thinking.

I temporarily lost my boundaries and became a snarling, whip-cracking villain. A chorus of moans and groans from the audience let me know they didn't like the role I played or the way I played it. In my mind that meant they didn't like me, a tough spot to be in for a people-pleaser.

On the long, lonely drive back to California from that workshop I felt cut off from all human contact. I could only talk to myself, wondering why the person I had become on the stage was so different from the person I wanted to be.

Never knowing just what love was, I had opted for the next best thing — respect. Suddenly, after those few minutes on a stage in Salt Lake City, the reality came through to me that others did not agree with me about the role I'd played in life.

If you consider participation in a psychodrama group, it would be wise to attend one in a residential setting or in the company of a trusted friend who can be with you for a while after leaving the group. It is not uncommon in the early stages of self-disclosure to feel despondent after first baring one's inner being to a room full of strangers.

My own case is a good example of why support is important. Lacking support or an appropriate place of healing after returning home to California, I let my experience of psychodrama drive me into a temporary retreat from my search for self. My life went flat. I couldn't see any destination on my horizon. It seemed all I could do was hope that if I went on, a day at a time, the quality of my life would improve with my own willingness to change.

And that's what happened. Something about the group experience fascinated me as the flame of a candle draws a moth. I'd had a peek into Pandora's box and felt compelled to know more about what went on inside me.

Encounter Groups

The encounter group is exactly what the name implies. People encounter each other as honestly and specifically as they can, trying to see themselves as they are seen by others.

They talk about feelings instead of thoughts. They learn to listen with their bodies and let their bodies be a major element in their communication with others. The process draws its style from a number of techniques, including psychodrama, Gestalt, body therapy and what some people call "touchy/feely" exercises.

The goals of an encounter group are:

1. To help us understand that we can come out from behind our masks and be ourselves through a process of open and honest communication with others.

2. To interact with others and hear them report their feelings about our interactions with them.
3. To heighten our awareness of the here and now and give
   up the denial and avoidance that goes with games of yes-
   terday and tomorrow.

Encounter and other interaction groups offer us a testing
ground for being who we might have been had we grown up in
a positive and nurturing environment. It is a place where we
learn we can neither destroy another human being nor be de-
stroyed by them in the course of human interaction.

Most of all, we learn that each of us is responsible for our
own feeling habits and we are reminded that "sticks and stones
may break our bones but names will never hurt us." We learn
that we can choose, or at least manage, the feelings that are
triggered in us as we interact with others.

My introduction to encounter groups came in the late 1960s
when some hailed it as the beginning of a new culture. William
C. Schutz, a guru of the human potential movement, summed
up the promise of encountering in the title of his book
Joy. (2) Enthusiasts of the new "encounter culture" spoke of a
new way of life as an "expansion and reintegration of body,
mind and soul."

Maybe so, but that wasn't how I experienced it when I encountered "encountering" some two years after my psychodrama incident. I smacked head-on into a big bundle of frustration
and pain. Once again I ran into the reality that my image of
myself was not consistent with the image others held of me.

My biggest problem then was my reliance on verbosity and
intellectualization as a means of communication. For years I'd
made my way as a talker, getting things done in law enforcement,
management and sales by either the power of authority or the
power of manipulation. I'd been a great talker but a poor listener.

In the encounter groups, talking failed me in my efforts to
make myself known to others. I gave only lip service to humility.
At work and at play I'd only mingled with go-getters of the
"better than" category. I'd taken it for granted that superior
doing was the mark of a superior being. "Conceited" was a
word that often came my way in those early days of my encountering. What didn't come my way was any of the hugging
that made up the closing celebration of an encounter marathon.

What I got instead was a "mirroring" of my aloofness, arrogance and narcissism. I came face to face with a reality I couldn't deny. I had to recognize that my way of being with people didn't serve my desire for their approval. I wanted to be accepted by them but had no concept of normal human relationships. As a result I suffered repeated rejection from others as I played my games in groups. Only some unexplainable drive kept me going on after the junkie in a Synanon group jeered, "You bombastic asshole."

It was a harsh experience in ego reduction — a beneficial one. Some of us need stronger medicine than others. At that time I had to learn the differences between pride and arrogance, assertiveness and aggressiveness, intention and compulsion, vision and grandiosity.

Today's beginners on the path of personal growth are offered gentler confrontation of their dysfunctional traits and characteristics than came my way in my earliest efforts at self-discovery. In ACoA and CoDA groups, people can discover their "differentness" from others without harsh confrontation. They can pace themselves, free of the resentment and rebellious anger I felt when others offered gratuitous advice on what I ought to do. In ACoA or CoDA groups you decide what is right for you to do.

Healthy Groups

Today you can find any number of self-discovery groups that encourage healthy human interaction and provide a means of "mirroring" to help you see yourself as others see you. In them you will find an opportunity to better understand yourself and the dynamics of your relationships with others.

Some marks of a healthy group are:

1. Interaction between group members is open and honest, emphasizing feelings rather than intellectualization. Self-responsibility is established by making statements instead of asking questions and by sending "I" messages in conversation rather than accusatory "You" messages.
2. Attention is focused on the present. Talking about the way it used to be and wishing how it might be in the future are avoidances of the present business. Look for

groups that focus on the business at hand, which is
learning to be authentic and autonomous right now.
3. Appropriate nonsexual touching is permitted and
encouraged, especially hugging. Healthy physical
expressions of affection are usually absent from the
homes of dysfunctional families but can be learned in
a supportive group.

The protective atmosphere of a healthy encounter group can
provide you with a greater sense of autonomy and a higher
level of comfort in your relationships outside the group. And
this comfort in human relationships is much of what recovery
from co-dependency is all about.

Transactional Analysis Groups

A major benefit of participation in a TA group is the opportunity to become a trained observer of your own personality at
work as you interact with others. As your understanding of *you*
increases so will your understanding of others. As your knowledge of effective communication skills increases, so will the
effectiveness of your interactions with others.

Your capacity to develop and enjoy healthy relationships will
be enlarged in direct proportion to your willingness to be in
charge of your personality as you interact with others in your
TA group. Appropriate use of TA knowledge and skills has
helped many people manage both their internal and external
affairs more effectively.

A Three-Part Model Of Personality
And Co-dependency

Your first task in a TA group is to learn to identify the three
parts of your personality known as *Parent*, *Adult* and *Child*.

The Parent in you thinks, feels and acts like a parent. At times
it can be demanding and critical and at other times it can be
nurturing and supportive.

The Adult in you is your human computer used in solving
problems or making decisions. It is theoretically capable of the
objectivity of an electronic computer, but that objectivity can be

messed up if the Adult is unduly influenced by Parentlike or Childlike thinking or feeling.

The Child in you thinks, feels and acts as you did in your childhood. If you were fortunate enough to have grown up in a functional, supportive family that provided a lot of permission to be yourself, the Natural Child in you can be imaginative, spontaneous and open in your relationships with others. If not, the Child in you may be either rebellious or compliant.

Wherever co-dependents meet there is much talk about the Child Within or the "free and precious child." Be aware here that the term "Child" is used differently by different people in different groups. There are both differences and similarities in the way it is defined by Charles Whitfield and by Eric Berne.

Whitfield: *"The Child within refers to that part of us which is ultimately alive, energetic, creative and fulfilled; it is our Real Self — who we truly are."* (3)

Berne: *"An archaic ego state. The Adapted Child follows parental directives. The natural Child is autonomous."* (4)

So the Child in TA terms encompasses both a Natural Child, similar to Whitfield's concept, and an Adapted Child with the adaptations being either passive or aggressive.

The Self-defeating Parent

The Parent is the motivating force that sabotages our chance for good feelings about ourselves. In our internal dialogue the Parent voice criticizes the Child within us and triggers the bad feelings that go with low self-esteem.

It is the critical Parent voice that is never satisfied with our efforts to get ahead or get along with others. It tells us we "ought to" do more.

We sabotage our potential for well-being when we let our minds be dominated by negative messages from childhood. We beat ourselves down and sabotage our chances for happiness when we let these outdated, toxic Parent messages govern our thought process and our emotions.

The hope for pleasant relationships is also sabotaged if we let Critical Parent habits intrude in our interactions with others.

Gruffness, finger-jabbing, and authoritarian behavior almost guarantee resentment or rebellion on the part of others.

Feedback in a good TA group will let you know how much you are letting the Parent part of you influence your thinking about yourself or your communication style. If you feel low after leaving your group, the chances are you have been overly self-critical, a Parent trait. If you regularly get into hassles with others in the group, there's a good chance you are coming from your Critical Parent.

In a TA group you will learn many ways to modify your Parent thinking and Parent behavior to gain greater peace of mind and happier human connections. Giving up inappropriate Parent influences on your current way of being is a major step toward autonomy.

Autonomy And The Integrated Adult

When uncontaminated by dysfunctional thinking habits, the Adult in you has the capacity of objective reality-testing, problem-solving, and decision-making. In a TA group that capacity will frequently be tested. Your peers will say "Use your Adult."

They will be telling you that at this moment they perceive you as being unduly influenced by some old negative Parent or Child tapes. They will be suggesting you exercise your autonomy and think, feel or do that which is appropriate to your current well-being instead of reacting with old dysfunctional habits.

However, not all childhood learning is inappropriate or dysfunctional in the exercise of our current affairs. Certain Parent and Child messages are appropriate to our well-being in adulthood. Ideally, they are integrated into our Adult ego state so we may be objective and effective in our thoughts and actions while also displaying the charm and openness of a child or exercising moral and ethical responsibility.

Early in his theorizing, Eric Berne suggested that the Adult part of human personality might also include the terms "pathos" (feelings of pity or compassion) and "ethos" (moral qualities such as courage, sincerity, loyalty and reliability). He wrote, ". . . this means that anyone functioning as an Adult should ideally exhibit three kinds of tendencies: personal attractiveness and responsiveness, objective data-processing, and ethical responsibility." (5)

In a TA group your peers will help you recognize moods or behaviors that seem to be unduly influenced by childhood programming. They can also help you make sound decisions about your choice of new life directions that reflect your desire for increasing autonomy and self-dependency.

The Co-dependent Child

It's too bad we don't all grow out of our co-dependent scripts the same way we grow out of our childhood clothes. But most of us don't. Few of us are blessed with the kind of parental or social permission that encourages attitudinal and emotional maturity. We become adults with a part of the Child in us still bound to the family rules that governed our attitudes and actions when we were young.

When these rules prove dysfunctional to us as adults, life turns sour. We are faced with the problem of updating our belief system and rewriting our co-dependent scripts.

In a TA group we have the opportunity to identify the child-like thoughts, emotions and behaviors that are not appropriate to our current well-being. We also find we have the privilege of receiving feedback from our peers about our childlike behaviors that negatively affect our interactions with them. We can resurrect the feelings of shame, guilt, rage and fear we stuffed down in childhood in the safe, warm and caring atmosphere of a healthy group.

Our challenge in a TA group is to track down the roots of our childlike, co-dependent ways, to decide in favor of more Adult functioning and to practice our newly chosen self-dependency. With the roots of our dysfunctional patterns exposed, we can get on with reparenting the co-dependent Child in us and updating our belief systems in ways appropriate to increased well-being.

Four Benefits From A TA Group

Self-understanding is essential to moving from co-dependency to self-dependency. As you move in that direction, the major benefits of participating in a TA group are:

1. Recognition of the Parent and Child influences on your thoughts, moods and behaviors and how they contami-

nate the potential of your Adult for objective problem-solving and decision-making. (Structural Analysis)

2. Increased awareness of the self-defeating style in which you may be interacting with others and how you can make constructive changes in your communication habits. (Transactional Analysis)

3. Identification of the co-dependent games you continue to play with others despite the bad feeling payoffs that go with them. (Game Analysis)

4. Acknowledgment of the co-dependent script that evolves from growing up in an alcoholic or otherwise dysfunctional family system. (Life Script Analysis)

This all may seem complicated to you now, but don't worry about it. Remember you'll be "doing TA" a step at a time. Noting how others use their Adult in sorting out data and deciding on appropriate action will help you do the same. In a TA group you will receive both helpful information and caring support as you undergo the transition from Child co-dependency to Adult self-dependency.

One of the greatest benefits to be gained in a TA group is a feeling of participation and belonging. Participating with others in a team effort to enrich the life experience of everyone in the group as they pursue autonomy is a wonderful exercise in self-actualization and being all that you can be. (For information about TA groups see Resources at the end of the book.)

Weekend Workshops

Workshops lasting a weekend or a few days give you things you can't get in any other kind of growth experience. You can dig inside yourself deeper than in a one-hour therapy group. You can let your feelings go without the restraints you might feel in a 12-Step group or at a seminar. You can nurture and be nurtured. You can indulge yourself in intimacy with others. You can practice being you. You can feel the strongly centered feeling that comes from authentic and autonomous behavior.

In the working time available in a weekend workshop you can live your new beginnings. Like an actress or actor trying out for a new play, you can test yourself in new roles. You can be outrageous or sulk alone in a corner.

You can act out your feelings while you feel them. You can make mistakes and be protected. You can expose the wounds of childhood abuse and not be scorned or shamed by others. You can experience the difference between aloneness and loneliness and know you never have to be lonely again except by choice.

Spending a weekend engulfed in a higher level of consciousness can be a psychic happening that widens the gateway to successful living. We can peek into the future and envision ourselves as one of those people Eric Berne had in mind when he wrote, "For certain fortunate people there is something that transcends all classifications of behavior, and that is awareness; something which rises above the programming of the past, and that is spontaneity; and something that is more rewarding than games, and that is intimacy." (6)

Bodywork Groups

Bodywork means just what it says. It is a collective term that includes any number of physical manipulations, techniques or exercises designed to promote awareness of the mind/body connection and promote greater cooperation between the two. Some of it we can do on our own: reflexology, acupressure and self-massage. Other work, the kind that goes deep into tissue to release the muscle-memories of childhood pain, should only be trusted to the hands of a certifiably trained practitioner.

Some bodywork is pleasurable and some is pure pain, though with a goal of ultimately being helpful. Some practitioners work with you on the issues triggered when the body-envelope is pulled, twisted or pushed out of its usual or normal state. Others will not. They leave it up to you to draw your own conclusions or encourage you to consult a psychotherapist or counselor for answers to questions arising from your emotional reactions to their bodywork.

The direct correlation between the body/mind connection and human well-being has been under discussion since ancient times. If you choose to explore bodywork as an adjunct to your recovery program, do begin with a discipline that has been around more than a little while and has established standards for its teachers. And do get information from a source you trust before putting your body/mind connections into the hands of a stranger.

In a bioenergetics workshop I first recognized the connection between my injunctions and certain "trigger points" in my body. In bioenergetics the theory is that there is no split between mind and body. Bioenergetics founder Alexander Lowen wrote, "To know who one is, an individual must be aware of what he feels. He should know the expression on his face, how he holds himself, and the way he moves. Without this awareness of bodily feeling and attitude, a person becomes split into a disenchanted body." (7)

In a bodywork session a therapist dug her thumbs deep into my rib cage and said, "Wow — you've got body armor like an armadillo." Under the skin of my back she found little nodules, collecting points for the thousands of feelings locked away for years in response to the demands of my macho script. When she bore down on those points I hurt, physically and emotionally. And when she released the pressure of those iron thumbs I felt relief, physically and emotionally.

Putting together some new knowledge of my body and the life-script information in my head, I was able to connect certain body feelings with my Claudia-Black-like injunctions: "Don't Talk, Don't Feel and Don't Touch."

Don't Talk

In my family the rule was either "Hold your tongue" or "Grit your teeth and bear it." I was also told repeatedly to stick out my chin and look like a man.

As an adult I had no idea that the habit of tightening my jaw muscles under stress had affected the form of my face where the jaw muscles hinged. I didn't know that a trained observer could see a slight bulge on each side of my jaws.

One experienced bioenergetics practitioner certainly saw it. I felt very calm and confident in his group and doubted he would see any tension spots in my body. Wrong. He came around behind where I was seated on the floor and reached down to put a hand on each side of my jaw. It hurt. I gritted my teeth fiercely resisting the pressure of his vise-like grip.

Stepping back, he snapped his thumbs away and released his grip. I sat still, numb for a moment. Then a sob came choking out of me like wind rushing up from a deep cave. After that I cried for half an hour. The physical pain had left but some pain of the soul kept me sobbing.

My workshop leader said nothing. It was not his custom to explain either his actions or the emotional release his manipulations provoked. He moved on and left me to make what I would of the experience.

It didn't take long to learn that when I felt my jaw clamped tight something wrong was going on in my thinking process. It was a reminder that my "Don't talk" injunction was at work and I was letting an old family rule interfere with my functioning in the here and now.

You might check yourself out on this. The next time you feel your jaws jammed tight for no apparent reason, check out the thoughts in your mind. Letting your jaws relax could help you straighten out your thoughts. Or straightening out the thoughts might help you relax your jaws and get rid of the tension in your body. Either way is a therapeutic contribution to your body/mind connection.

Don't Feel

This injunction can have two different meanings. When most people talk about feelings they mean emotions. Ask a person how he feels and the chances are he'll tell you about his state of mind. He'll use words like: fine, sad, okay, worried, angry or whatever best describes his mood.

Ask him how his mood feels in his body and he'll say, "What do you mean?" Press him and maybe he'll tell you about a few aches and pains. He may even tell you he feels down because his body aches or make some other link between his physical feelings and his mood. Other than that, he has no concept of body/mind connections or the signals from his body that might affect his state of mind.

What I'm suggesting here is that you become more aware of the difference between *psychic numbness* and *physical numbness*. There are times it may seem impossible to express your emotions or thoughts in words. Chances are at those times your body-feelings system may also shut down. You may be completely unaware that your gut muscles are as tight as the strings on a violin or the muscles behind your shoulders are as bunched up as those of a weightlifter.

Both Rowena and I had more than our share of sustained
stress in childhood, the kind that results in mind splitting off
from body. We both lived with fear for a long time. Her fear
was a specific reaction to her father's drunken rages. Her reminder of it in adulthood is a cold spot in her stomach.

My fears were more general. I lived in constant fear that I
would be rejected by others. I had to constantly adjust to
strangers when I was moved to another boarding school, a
house in a strange neighborhood or a different school. My adult
connection with those childhood fears is a drawn-up feeling in
my belly muscles, muscle spasms behind my shoulders or tight--
ness in my jaws.

Now, knowing that muscular tension may be a reminder of
childhood stress, shifting our mental energies from the past to
the present usually provides relief from physical tension. When
it doesn't, a few deep breaths will get us back on the track of
wholeness with body and mind working in harmony.

It's possible you will find your own way to an increased awareness of your body/mind connections. Doing so will increase
your chances of escape from the "Don't Feel" injunctions that
may be keeping you from being a fully-functioning person. Autonomy means freedom from physical as well as mental tension.

Don't Touch

A person who has suffered physical or sexual abuse in childhood will probably need more than a self-help program to become comfortable with physical contact. People who have suffered such abuse are usually best served in their recovery by
seeking help from a therapist skilled in that area.

However, some of us with "Don't Touch" injunctions simply
grew up in nontouching environments. Perhaps we didn't get
the holding or hugging we needed as infants. Or perhaps later
we ran into strong family rules against touching. Sometimes
the message was specific: "Don't touch . . . (sister, brother,
mother, father) like that." Sometimes it was modeled by parents
who never touched each other in our presence. Or if they did,
sly grins and giggles implied things were going on that we
weren't supposed to know about.

My childhood memory bank doesn't have any recollections of
being held or hugged. In the days of my infancy mothers did not

breast-feed their children. We got Eagle brand canned milk served in a bottle.

In the boarding schools where I lived, they told us little boys who "touched" themselves would go crazy. Later, after returning home to live with my brother and half-sister, one warning about playing "Doctor" ended our attempts to know more about the differences between little girls and little boys. I never saw any touching or kissing around the house.

My first gentle massage brought me sadness, the kind that aches through the body. Continued bodywork and some practice of mutual massage brought me to a point where I could enjoy the warmth of nonsexual hugs with Rowena, something she had often longed for in the past.

A good place to check out your own position on touching or being touched is at almost any 12-Step meeting. The close of a meeting often includes a lot of hugging, some appropriate and some not. If you are not comfortable with being hugged or giving hugs, it is okay to say so. This is a matter of respect for your personal boundaries as well as those of others. It is also a matter of choicemaking, being autonomous and breaking the co-dependent habit of "going along with the gang."

Check out your motivation for hugging members of the opposite sex. Be clear with yourself about the difference between platonic intimacy and sexual innuendo. To inappropriately hug another is a form of self-sabotage that invites a put-down.

Some bodywork might help you loosen up a bit. It is also a part of the process of self-discovery and a way to make improvements in the body/mind connection. In the fully-functioning human being the body and mind are partners in a joint venture dedicated to higher levels of well-being.

Sharon Fogarty, a recovery counselor and consultant, says, "Gentle bodywork with someone who has an understanding of body/mind connections has been helpful to me in my own recovery." She also adds a warning: "People physically or sexually abused in childhood should be very careful about heavy bodywork. It could trigger lots of emotion, stuff out of the past. Lots of compassion and support need to be available."

So do be encouraged to learn more about how your body reflects your temperament and personality. But keep a level head as you choose the practitioner or therapist who will help you better understand the unique entity that is you.

Life Skills Training Groups

Successful recovery from co-dependency demands more than a change of attitude. It calls for increased effectiveness in life skills, the "how to's" of self-management and successful inter- actions with others. It takes action to change dreams into reality.

Here's how that goes:

Lou Ellen gains a good understanding of her personality struc- ture in a transactional analysis group. She realizes the influence her domineering father had on her life script and on her ten- dency to play the role of a Victim.

She's seen diagrams outlining the Passive Child part of her personality that dictates her submissiveness. Intellectually she understands her problem but the habits of assertiveness are almost unknown to her. In an assertiveness training class she is patiently led through a series of exercises leading to new behav- ioral skills that permit the expression of her needs.

By practicing in group she gains confidence and slowly learns to express herself to others. At home, with her husband's coop- eration, she begins to state her needs in a forthright manner instead of hinting at them. She takes the car to the garage for minor repairs, something she has previously dreaded doing. She gets a part-time job, partly to bolster her self-esteem and partly because the money is welcome.

For Lou Ellen, self-understanding only added to her self- knowledge. It didn't change much for her in how she related to other people. However, when she finally learned actual skills to take advantage of that knowledge, she found she could put her self-knowledge into action.

Similarly, in his CoDA group, Spencer gains a great deal of knowledge about how he got to be the aggressive co-dependent he is. From this he sees that he'd like to be different. He knows that unless he can mellow out with his employees, he's in trouble with his career. But he doesn't know how to translate this knowledge into action.

In a corporate communications training class Spencer learns how his gruff voice and dictatorial gestures create resentment in those under his charge. In this class he practices new vocal tones and learns to make gentle, open-handed gestures. The people who work for him notice his change and relax a little, more comfortable in his presence. Productivity in Spencer's unit goes up and so do his chances for promotion.

Constructive Change — Constructive Action

Constructive change comes only when constructive action is taken. The plumber who would be a carpenter must do more than gain an understanding of carpentry. He must learn the use of tools new to him and the skills appropriate to his change of calling. So it is with recovering co-dependents as they move along into new territories of maturation and adult development.

Suppose you disembarked today from a British Airways jet at Heathrow Airport near London. You pick up a car at a rental agency. You are dismayed to discover the steering wheel is on the right side of your car, which is the wrong side for you. At that point survival dictates your immediate change in certain actions involved with driving.

That's the way it is for most of us in early recovery. We are faced with learning new skills. Much of what was "right" in the past is "wrong" or inappropriate in the present. Attitudes and actions that we assumed were functional may prove painfully dysfunctional. Unless irrevocably committed to denial we wake up to a new awareness that much of our past operational style is out of synch with our striving for well-being. If we are to synchronize our energies and our dreams with our new goals, both new thinking and new living skills are in order.

This is particularly true concerning the communication skills necessary to our functioning as self-dependent people. What psychiatrist Ronald Shlensky has to say about communications training is especially relevant to co-dependents. He says, "The entire quality of life can be vastly improved by learning to communicate effectively — especially in conflict-ridden situations." (8)

Always keep in mind that we weren't born co-dependent. It's a way of life we learned, one that can be replaced with new learning. Learning new life skills will help get your thinking/feeling/perceiving/behaving system into appropriate balance.

Some skills training groups or classes that can be helpful to anyone seeking increased effectiveness in managing their lives are:

- Assertiveness Training
- Interpersonal Communications Training
- Public Speaking or Toastmasters

- Parent Effectiveness Training
- Supervisory or Management Training

Therapy Groups

Therapy groups are generally different from personal growth, self-development, or self-help groups in three ways:

1. They always have a leader.
2. The leader (therapist) has met the standards of a university, a governing body and/or a state board of certification.
3. A diagnosis or interview is usually conducted by the therapist before an individual begins group treatment. If your costs are to be paid by an insurance company your presenting problem will have to be classified and coded for the convenience of the insurance company's computers. (Co-dependency has yet to be classified as a diagnosis by those who rule on such matters. How you will be classified is at the discretion of your therapist.)

People usually arrive in group therapy as a consequence of:

1. Admission to an inpatient or outpatient treatment program for substance abuse.
2. Admission to a program for treatment of co-dependency. Inpatient treatment for co-dependency is starting to become available at a few hospitals and residential recovery centers.
3. Referral to an ongoing therapy group by a counselor, psychologist or psychiatrist. Such referral is not usually made until a patient or client has undergone some individual treatment.
4. Individual choice. When people hurt enough, get tired of staying in the miserable rut of severe co-dependency or discover that other people are enjoying the benefits of recovery while they are not, they often seek groups that offer hope for change.

Choosing A Group Leader

Who is best suited to lead you along the path from discontent to self-fulfillment? That's not an easy question to answer. It is up to you to choose your paid-for mentor, teacher or therapist.

Before you make that choice, get to know what you can about the person you think might best help you in your growth. Talk to others. Competence is not guaranteed by degrees, licenses or certificates. Successful experience in helping people, as marked by word-of-mouth reputation, is more important than fancy flyers or scrolled ads in the Yellow Pages.

These are the qualities I would look for in a group leader:

1. An empathy born of personal experience in the search for autonomy or escape from co-dependency.
2. The kind of Tough Love that would confront my denial or resistance without judgmental putdowns, scorn or sarcasm.
3. The patience to let me be my sometimes obtuse and unreasonable self without demeaning me.
4. An aura of competence and confidence free of any "sales pitches" or false promises about the future.
5. Provision of an atmosphere of protection and trust so I would feel free to disclose my inner being without fear of being "zapped" by the leader or others in the group.
6. A modeling of autonomy or recovery by an absence of "shoulds" or "ought to's." I want no part of anyone who doesn't "walk their talk."
7. The willingness to teach me enough so I can learn to handle my co-dependency problems outside the group and "graduate" from it in reasonable time.
8. The sensitivity to respond to group members as unique individuals requiring different approaches to their individual needs and problems.
9. The patience to actively listen, to mirror or to give feedback until my meaning is clear, instead of making assumptions.
10. The expertise to deal with me as a thinking/feeling person. Sometimes I need to experience my feelings and

sometimes I need to intellectually understand what is going on with me.

11. The wisdom to know what can and cannot be changed. Sometimes I learn as much from what doesn't happen in the group as what does. Sometimes the Parent-Child conflict within me is so violent I don't hear what is said to me. I don't want to be forced to move at the leader's pace. I'd rather be trusted to work through my stuck places on my own or come back to them later when my mind has cleared.

That is quite a list to consider for a hurting, confused co-dependent in search of a *master teacher*. Nevertheless, working at being selective is better than letting your fate be decided by a flip of the coin or an impulsive whim.

Whatever you do, don't seek the perfect leader. There are none. And your quest for perfection inevitably leads to your criticizing or rejecting them for their perceived faults, a counterproductive continuation of the games co-dependents play.

ᴖ6 ᴖ

Redeciding
Life Directions

*At about the same time we were looking at the decisions we made in
childhood, we began to realize that if a child made a decision, he could,
and often did, change it later and* **not necessarily in therapy.** *(author's emphasis)*

— **Robert L. Goulding, MD and
Mary McClure Goulding, MSW**

In this chapter we'll explore changing our co-dependent scripts
by taking a new look at the early childhood decisions underlying
them. We'll examine the reality that we each have the power to
redecide them in favor of a more autonomous way of life.

Your Power To Redecide

Bob Goulding, originator of redecision therapy, regarded Eric
Berne as a friend and great teacher. However, Bob disagreed
with him concerning the source of power that makes personal
change possible. Berne believed that power to be in the therapist. Bob believes it is you who have the power to change, to
redecide your life directions.

In *The Power Is In The Patient*, Goulding writes, "I see the power as being in the patient, not in the therapist, and that the therapist's real job is to *allow* the patient to find his own power . . ." (1) Finding my own power has certainly worked for me. I believe it will work for you too, as you go about making the redecisions that will better your life.

There are three kinds of *redecisions* to consider: *spontaneous*, *guided* and *reprogrammed* redecisions.

Spontaneous Redecisions

Spontaneous redecisions can be likened to spontaneous combustion. There is a long-time smoldering and then a sudden spark or flame. Some people can just stand the heat of life so long and then they explode into a new form. They become "born again." They may have a dramatic, overnight spiritual awakening or other "mind-blowing" experience. People coming back from a near-death experience have also reported a sudden change of values and outlook on life resembling a redecision experience.

Among those who have experienced spontaneous redecisions are the "burnouts" and "dropouts" who get tired of straddling the fence and dramatically change their life directions. For one reason or another, sometimes unknown to them, they feel compelled toward a new destiny. For example, Richard Cornuelle was an executive vice-president of the National Association of Manufacturers. He had a secretary he called his "girl," had his shoes shined every day and lived at the University Club.

One day he walked out. He writes, "I wish I could say I left the NAM (National Association of Manufacturers) and the buttoned-down way of living that went with it for some, conscious reason. But I didn't. I left because I had to. Something inside me simply went on strike." (2)

It would be a rare co-dependent who had never experienced the feeling of wanting to "go out on strike." However, having that happen by virtue of a spontaneous redecision is all too rare. We can hardly rely on it as an escape from our life scripts. To do so is as futile as waiting for Santa Claus.

Guided Redecisions (Redecision Therapy)

Guided redecisions are just what the name implies. They are accomplished with the assistance of a professional guide skilled in the process of redecision therapy as taught by Bob and Mary Goulding at the Western Institute of Group and Family Therapy. Bob and Mary are dedicated to the belief that each of us has the power to redecide our early childhood decisions and free ourselves from the negative injunctions that keep us bound in co-dependency. We can give up our *games* and *rackets*, cast off our roles as Persecutors, Victims or Rescuers, and modify our life scripts in the direction of autonomy. (3)

Every one of us has the power to change even though that power may be dormant. The redecision therapist can help us track down our early childhood decisions, identify our injunctions, re-experience the childhood feelings that go with them and redecide new life directions. For the co-dependent this means giving up unhealthy other-directed childhood programming in favor of healthy self-directed programming.

The redecisioning process is an intellectual/emotional "working through" of barriers to growth. With the help of a therapist a subject moves back through time and relives certain childhood scenes or events, bringing up buried memories and emotions. There is a sudden awareness that the past does not have to rule the present and — in what can appear to be a moment of magic — a redecision is made.

Time after time I've seen the surprised, childlike look on a person's face as he or she looked at Bob or Mary and said, "I don't have to do that anymore." The impasse to autonomy is broken. They suddenly see a way out of the misery of dysfunctional scripts and roles they decided on in early childhood.

After coming back to the here and now the client is invited to make a new decision. An appeal is made to the objective, problem-solving, decision-making Adult part of the self.

"What are you willing to do about that?"

"Got any ideas how to fix that?"

"How would you rather be, now that you know you have a choice?"

Questions like these are reminders that you have the power of redecision. Answering them is an exercise in autonomy and the first step forward in your new directions.

Exhilarating as a redecision experience may be, it is only the beginning. Lifetime habits of thinking, feeling, perceiving and behaving will need to be examined for how they serve or fail to serve one's new goals. Some may be kept, some modified and some discarded.

The co-dependent belief system is burdened with psychological garbage that impedes the Adult capacity for making appropriate decisions. The guided redecision process is one step in
the work of getting rid of garbage. Another step is reprogramming, a method that can lead to major redecisions on its own or
can reinforce guided redecisions.

Reprogrammed Redecisions

Reprogramming as a means of restructuring personality is
not a new concept. The *Bhagavadgita,* revered for 2,000 years by
Hindus, describes the concept of *samskara* which means essen-
tially that *thoughts* repeated many times lead to *actions* repeated
many times. Personality is a collection of *samskaras.* And every
thought can be changed.

In terms of redecision therapy this means we are the product
of thoughts which reinforce our childhood decisions. Repeated
over and over, they reinforce our commitment to a co-dependent script.

However, we can rethink our childhood thoughts, redecide
our childhood decisions and reprogram our childhood programming. In every thought there is an opportunity to make a new
choice. Just as a *samskara* is built up through repeated thought
and word and action, it can be unbuilt and rebuilt through
repeated thought and word and action of the opposite kind.

Samskara has appeared in the Western world as "positive thinking" or "self-management." About 1920 Coue-ism, a self-help
method of autosuggestion, developed by French psychotherapist
Emile Coue, swept this country. Thousands of people, my mother among them, went about repeating to themselves throughout
their day, *"Every day in every way, I'm getting better and better."* In the
early 1950s Norman Vincent Peale turned our minds to the
power of positive thinking. Not many years later Maxwell Maltz
brought us the combination of positive thinking and positive
self-imaging known as psycho-cybernetics.

All these methods of mental management work — for some
people, some of the time. For a few they work all the time.

They worked for me too, much of my life, while I was striving
toward fulfillment of what others defined as success or higher
social status. They didn't work for me when I began my inner
yearning for freedom from co-dependency.

Positive thinking helped me create a self which performed well. But it only changed my lifestyle. Beneath the surface I still lacked faith in myself and suffered the fears of rejection and failure that went with my old co-dependent script.

Giving Up Old Scripts

After I learned about life scripts and injunctions I understood why positive thinking and positive self-imaging alone hadn't worked for me. Over a 25-year period I changed careers four times before I broke through my "Don't Make It" injunction. My freedom came not through positive thinking but by realizing that in our family nobody was supposed to surpass my step-father. With my hidden fears of rejection and disapproval re-solved, I was able to live up more fully to the positive thinking images I created for my life.

With some understanding of my injunctions and recognition of them as voices from the past, I was able to begin changing the feeling habits connected to them. I had to do that before I could exercise the power of choice. Having redecided in favor of autonomy I was able to get on with living free and clear of my old, dysfunctional thinking/feeling habits — a condition I call happiness.

The first step in reprogramming one's dysfunctional habits is to acknowledge the power of choice in the matter of feelings. An example is the feeling of rejection that sometimes comes when we make a mistake or suffer failure in the eyes of others. We "rubberband" to past experiences and re-feel childhood feelings of doing something incorrectly and being called bad.

Sam, a salesman, loses a sale and feels the same old feeling of being rejected that he felt in childhood. He may think of himself as a bad salesman even though his customer may have changed his mind for any one of a thousand rational reasons.

Sam thinks, "Boy, there must really be something wrong with me." Sometimes he says this to himself and sometimes he even says it to his sales manager. He confuses his doing with his being. He is totally unaware of the old voice in his mind that says, "What's the matter with you? You stupid kid, can't you ever do anything right?"

The voice is from the past but the feelings of rejection that come with the loss of his sale are in the present. His impulse is to quit selling, go get drunk or take a few days off. Sam doesn't know that if he could pinpoint his "Don't Make It" injunction he could say, "Okay. I lost a sale. I took all the appropriate steps to make that sale. Maybe I made a mistake. Maybe my prospect changed his mind for reasons he isn't saying. Now, how long do I want to feel bad: five minutes, five hours, or five days? How long do I want to feel bad because I felt rejected by my father?"

Hopefully, he will decide five minutes is enough time to wallow in misery and get on with making his next call. And hopefully, once you've learned to connect your feelings with your injunctions, you will do the same. You will choose to be in charge of your thoughts and feelings in the present rather than be blindly bound to your old thinking/feeling habits.

Connecting Your Present With Your Past

Accepting as reality the probability that most of what goes on with you in the present is influenced by childhood thinking/feeling habits is a gateway to autonomy. With the connection made between past and present, you are free to make choices about the way you want to think, feel and act in the present. You can update your life plan and be in charge of your recovery.

That's not something that gets done overnight, of course. It will go on bit by bit as you move along in the development of your new self-directed thinking/feeling habits. Instead of responding by habit you will find yourself more and more in charge of what you do, how you do it and how you feel about doing it. You will become increasingly competent in managing all your affairs, internal and external.

Like a playwright you can edit as you go along. You can cross out actions that don't lead to a happy ending. You can write in for yourself the role of a Comfortable Winner, one who thinks and feels by choice rather than by habit.

For example, in my old life script a strong theme was "Life's a struggle" and the injunction connected with that was "Don't make it." In my selling days sometimes I'd make a big sale, feel elated for a while then suffer pangs of guilt because it had been too easy. I discounted my competence and credited fate with my luck. I'd forget the hours of prospecting and planning that went into the sale. I defied my injunctions by being successful and then felt the same bad feelings I'd had in childhood when put down by my stepfather.

After I learned about injunctions I knew that, despite whatever success I had in the future, habitual bad feelings would crop up from time to time. When they did, I was prepared. I would review in my mind what I had done that contributed to my success. I'd give myself credit for my increasing competence and enjoy the results of having reprogrammed my belief system. The way that process goes is:

1. Recognize the Don'ts in your belief system (Don't Trust, Feel, Think, Be You, Make It, Grow Up, Enjoy Yourself, Be Important, Be Close, Belong, Be Well, Be Sane or just plain old Don't).
2. Identify the bad feelings (mad, bad or sad) that go with defiance of your injunctions.
3. Decide what feelings you'd prefer to have.
4. Make conscious choices of action appropriate to good thinking/feeling habits.
5. Get on with doing what needs to be done to fulfill desirable goals.
6. Give yourself positive strokes for acting like a Winner.

At the moment this may seem complicated but with time and practice, the process will become almost automatic. Repetition is fundamental to learning new thinking/feeling habits.

The next time you suffer a bad feeling, think of it as a choice. Be honest with yourself. Accept your responsibility for your feelings. Doing so will help you lessen the time spent in misery, increase your feel-good time and heighten your sense of self-dependency.

Once you've begun to think of your bad feelings as choices, you can move toward the reprogrammed redecisions you can make in the interests of exercising your right to enjoy life as a vibrant and autonomous human being.

More about how to use this reprogramming process to your advantage is outlined in a later chapter. For the moment let's take a deeper look at what goes on in the redecision experience. Understanding all you can about the dynamics of that process can help you in your own self-therapy or in deciding whether professional help is in order.

Experiencing A Guided Redecision

If you've ever awakened in the morning with a feeling that you suddenly can see your way clear to the solution of some troubling problem, you have some sense of the feeling that goes with making a redecision. Clarity, exhilaration and relief are the words that fit for me in describing that experience.

The example here describes my thinking/feeling redecision process of breaking free from a powerful "Don't Belong" injunction. This sense of alienation stemmed from my abandonment to a boarding school at about age four. Constantly moving from one house and school to another throughout childhood reinforced my perception of being a stranger in the world.

Let's look at the way I changed that perception:

The scene for this redecision experience is the Big Room at the Western Institute for Group and Family Therapy, housed in an old, rambling California ranch house. At one end of the room is a huge window overlooking the Pajaro Valley and the blues and greens of the Pacific Ocean.

At the other end of the room is Bob Goulding, seated in his aged armchair, his bare feet resting on a worn leather footstool. Alongside him Mary is standing by an easel with a huge blank newsprint pad, ready to diagram the dynamics of any transactions between the two of them and any one of us.

Between them is a long-playing tape recorder. It is "the cop on the beat." It is ready to confront our denials by playing back what we've just said if we try to avoid responsibility for our words.

Bob and Mary function as both teachers and therapists, delivering information and guidance to the person in the "hot seat." Step by step they lead or guide clients through an exploration of their life scripts, helping them find damaging injunctions and redecide their childhood decisions.

A redecision therapy group is a combination of one-on-one and interactive group therapy. After each engagement between therapist and client, questions are answered, group discussion goes on and whatever personal issues may have come up for any of the others in the group are dealt with.

On the day in question the lovely summer morning is in sharp contrast to the murky feelings in my gut as I sit among the 40 or so clients around the room. We are all trainees, learning redecision therapy for use in our work and lives.

As usual Bob says, "Who wants to work this morning?" This is an invitation to join the Inner Circle where the work goes on. Those in the Outer Circle will learn by observing.

With Bob and Mary there is no beating around the bush. They emphasize personal responsibility for everything that goes on with us, every thought and feeling. We say "I want . . . " or "I need . . . " rather than hinting at or suggesting what we'd like others to do for us.

Once someone in the Inner Circle indicates a willingness to work, Bob says, "What's in your foreground?" just as you might say to someone, "What's on your mind?" In effect Bob is saying, "I am here. I am willing to hear you. I am willing to share with you what I know about helping people change. I am willing to both confront you and support you in your efforts at becoming an autonomous person."

Each of us reports what is most pressing with us or what is going on in our minds that troubles us. It may be a problem we brought with us to the month-long training. It may be something that just pops up in the experience of tracking down our injunctions and exploring our life scripts.

I feel Bob looking at me. His big blue eyes seem to shine straight into my mind. He's read something in my body language that signals my inner turmoil. "What's with you, Joe?"

Suddenly I feel everyone looking at me, like the time in boarding school when I took the last piece of toast without knowing it was against the rules. I didn't know then I was supposed to sacrifice my needs for others.

I say to Bob, "Why don't you look after Betty first? She needs help more than I do." It's a manipulation I've used for years, getting myself off the spot by being "polite" and letting someone else go first.

Bob doesn't respond to my attempted manipulation of the circumstances. He says, "Betty can take care of herself. Do you want to work or don't you?"

I nod my head but can't get any words out. I want to deny or avoid any inference that I am anything less than Superman, always in control. But my hands betray me. They wander around in front of me as they always used to when I felt blocked and stupid.

My throat is almost too tight to talk but Bob gently urges me on. "What do you want to do with your hands, Joe?"

I look at Bob. I look at my hands. My gut muscles draw in. My body feels like it's in the grip of an octopus. My breath gets shallow. I'm on the spot. I feel exposed and, like many co-dependents, can only show my feelings in anger. I want to hit somebody or run away. The Parent voice in my head says, "There you go again, you stupid kid. Got yourself on the spot, didn't you?"

Bob persists. "Double up your fists, Joe."

I don't bother asking why. I've been watching Bob and Mary work for two weeks and know the incredible speed with which they read what is going on with poeple. I've learned to trust their instincts.

I double my fists. I feel the muscles gather behind my neck and at the back of my shoulders. I'm ready to fight.

"So who do you want to hit?"

"You." My voice escapes in a bellow. I'm surprised at the vehemence of my response. I've gone from apprehension to anger in a split second, a pattern that troubled me for years and still does now and then.

"Because?" The Gouldings never ask, "Why?" It invites too much denial and avoidance. "Because" calls for facts and reality.

"Because you made me feel stupid."

Bob smiles. "Who made you feel stupid, Joe?"

I grin. Some of the tension goes out of my body. My hands open. I know the rules and I take responsibility for my feelings. "I made me feel stupid."

Mary says, "How did you do that, Joe?"

"Coming here. Sitting out here like a jackass."

"Like everybody's looking at you?"

I have to think a moment. "Well, not exactly. I don't mind everybody looking at me sometimes. Teaching a class, doing a workshop. Sometimes I like being the center of attention."

Bob says, "What's different here? You said you felt stupid about coming here. What's that all about?"

Mary scrawls big letters with a broad-tipped marker on the blank sheet of newsprint beside her. "Don't Belong."

She asks, "You don't belong with all these professionals?" The wave of her hand includes the psychologists, psychiatrists, social workers and counselors in the group. "Pretty smart people."

She's got it. All my life I've felt stupid around people with advanced degrees or important titles. I always froze inside and tried acting wise by nodding my head and keeping my mouth shut.

I'm feeling the same way again as Mary questions me but I know I can't cop out by acting cool. My jaw locks again. My throat tightens. My hands wander but not in anger. They signal my feelings of helplessness.

Bob asks, "You have permission to be smart, Joe?"

I shake my head. In my house nobody could ever be as smart as my stepfather. Any attempt at being "equal to" was shot down with sarcasm.

Bob says, "So you're an outsider. You don't belong here with all these smart people?"

I'm still too choked up to talk so I nod.

"Your application form says you belong to Mensa."

I nod again.

"Takes a pretty high I.Q., doesn't it?"

Another nod. I don't tell him that I dropped out of Mensa because I didn't seem to fit in with smart people even though I'd passed their entry examinations.

"And you're working on your Master's now?"

"Yes, but I'm damn near 55."

Bob chides me. "Yes, but . . . ?"

I recognize my avoidance and "Yes, but" game-playing. "Yes. Seems silly, doesn't it?"

"Is that how it seems to you, Joe?" As usual Bob does not judge me but forces me into taking responsibility for my perceptions. Nor does he let me get away with having him answer for me.

"It seems silly in my head, like I know it isn't rational, but I have this feeling. Sometimes I just get cold in my gut when I feel like I'm left out. Like an intruder. Like I just don't belong."

"When's the last time you felt that way?"

Before I can answer Mary breaks in. "I don't think Joe gave us a contract."

She's right. I hadn't made a commitment to work, to be willing to work through my feelings and get back to the childhood

memories underlying that "left out" feeling and my "Don't Belong" injunction.

Bob says, "How about it, Joe? What do you want to change
about you?"

"Well, I guess I . . . " I'm interrupted.

"No guessing."

That brings a laugh from everyone in the room. We all know
specificity is the rule.

"I want to stop feeling left out and inferior when I'm around
professionals."

"Are you willing to do that?"

"God, yes. I'm tired of these left-out feelings."

"Are you willing to track down that 'Don't Belong' injunction?"

"Yes." I say it loud and clear because I know he'll ask me to do
it over unless he hears me put some power into my commitment.

With a contract committed to, Mary continues, "When's the
last time you had this cold feeling about being left out?"

"Last night. Everyone's up here in the Big Room. Dancing.
Singing. I'm down in the Barn, reading a book." The Barn is just
that, an old remodeled barn. Empty except for me it seems to be
about the end of everywhere.

"So everybody's in the Big Room having a good time and you
choose to be in the Barn. What are you saying to yourself?"

I blankly look at Mary and shrug. "I should have stayed in the
insurance business."

Mary laughs. "Did you hear the Parent in there?"

"Sure. I said 'I should have'."

Mary says, "And the Child in you? What's he saying?"

"Nothing. He's all choked up." I stare at the floor.

Mary says, "What's going on, Joe? Where are you? How old
are you?"

"Ten years old. I'm not sure. Ten or eleven. I'm at the play-
ground. All the other kids have been picked for the baseball
teams. The biggest one finally jerks his thumb at me and says,
'Well, guess we have to take him.' I smile like I'm happy but
inside I'm numb."

Mary's voice drops. "That hurts a little kid, doesn't it?"

I can't talk for a minute, too busy wiping tears out of my eyes.
"It sure does, still does." The anger comes back. I feel like an
angry little kid and my voice sounds that way. "I didn't like the
damn game anyway."

Mary says, "Is that a familiar feeling for you, feeling left out?"

"Sure." I know the tracking-down process so there's no need to go back through scene after scene of feeling left out in childhood.

That's how it had been, too, as an adult. My whole business life had been pushing myself ahead, getting myself into strange territory, bluffing my way along, sometimes even getting honors, but never feeling like I belonged.

A lucky toss of a discus had gained me a college education but I was a poor kid on a rich campus. I lived on dreams and my love for Rowena 'til I found out a few beers gave me protection from the not-belonging feelings.

In high school I'd walk to school in shirtsleeves despite the cold weather because I didn't have a sweater. I pretended I was conditioning for the track team. I made the basketball team but had to drop out because I didn't have money for gym shoes. I'd gone to seven different junior high schools because it was the Depression and we were always skipping out on our rent. We even moved one Christmas Eve.

I say to Mary, "It was always like that. Always moving away from one school to another, always feeling different, like there was something wrong with me."

Mary shakes her head. "What was it like when you were real little?"

"Same thing. My mother and father divorced when I was four. Judge put me in boarding homes. One weekend with mother, next with father. I don't know how many of those homes I lived in — three, maybe four. Never knew why I was there."

I hear a sob from somebody in the Outer Circle, probably someone caught up in their own childhood memories.

Another question from Mary. "How did you feel, being a little kid without a home?"

"I don't really know. Stuffed it, I guess. I made up a lot of stories. Read a lot. Pretended I was a hero. Wished I could be home. Just survived 'til I got to go home when mother remarried. I was seven or eight I guess."

"What was the worst part?"

"The teasing. My hair was long and curly. The kids always teased me. Called me sissy so I'd cry."

I sit, looking at Mary and Bob. I don't see them. I'm back into my childhood and am a scared, lonely little kid again. I feel the sadness, the loneliness of childhood. And I feel scared. I don't know why but I can feel it in my gut.

Bob sees it. "What's going on now, Joe? You look frightened. Where are you?"

"In the attic." My body felt cold, just as if I were a real five- or six-year-old alone in a big cold, spooky attic. "There was a cot up there. We got put up there if we were bad. This bigger kid held me out the window, said he'd drop me. Then he left me alone in the dark. Said the rats would get me."

Bob's voice lowers. "Then what happened?"

I shake my head. "Nothing. I just lay on the iron cot, listening for the rats and crying 'til I fell asleep."

"And how are you feeling all by yourself in that dark attic?"

"Lonely. Scared. Real lonely." By now I'm sobbing. "Awful lonesome."

A woman beside me starts to put her arm around me but Bob stops her in a kindly way. "No. Not yet. No rescuing. Let him feel his feelings."

He looks back at me. "Is that how you felt last night out in the Barn?"

I nod. Bob sits there and just looks at me. I start to ask a question but then something hits me and I'm mad, sad and happy all at the same time. Suddenly my mind is completely clear. My vision is restored. I've come to a thinking/feeling moment of truth.

I say, "Damn! You mean all these years I've been doing this to myself, reliving these old feelings by choice? Giving myself all these awful feelings?"

Bob says, "Yup."

It takes a few seconds for that to sink in. The Child in me bellows, "Well, hell, I don't have to do that any more."

Bob says, "How about your Adult, Joe? What does it say?"

I feel bouncy and all light inside but at the same time I recognize the seriousness of the question. I feel the vibration in my chest as the pitch of my voice drops to a lower key. I say, "I mean it. I don't have to let that sad little kid keep me from belonging anymore. It's my choice. I can belong if I choose to."

Everybody in the room shouts, "Of course."

That's the custom at the Western Institute when a redecision is made. It's external support for the Child within, positive strokes for redeciding the old tapes that bind folks to the past. It's also recognition that a person has exercised the full capacity of his Adult.

Mary says, "So what do you do now instead of feeling left out?"

I gulp in a big breath of air. "Remember I don't have to feel now like I did then." That's reinforcement for the redecision part that comes from the Child. "I'll get so competent in my field I won't have to bluff anymore." That's the Adult part of the redecision.

Mary says, "That sounds okay but pretty Adult. What are you going to do for the Child inside?"

"Oh." I slap my hand against my forehead. That's so typical of me to think like a grownup and forget the little kid in me. "I'll join the group in the Big Room and have some fun."

Bob smiles. "Okay. Now go around the room and tell each one of those professionals, 'I'm smart and I belong here.'"

I do. My stomach churns while I do it, but it strengthens my resolve to change my thinking/feeling habits about not belonging. I can hear a change in my vocal tones, a straightforwardness different from the puffery and braggadocio my voice projected for so many years when I posed as something I was not but always wanted to be. I know and feel at the same time that I am more "equal to" instead of "less than" among a bunch of specialists in the field of human behavior.

The feeling of self-confidence that came in the wake of that redecision experience is hard to describe but it has grown stronger over the years. It's totally on the other side of the coin from the feelings that went with my self-defeating co-dependency.

Another important learning that came out of my work with the Gouldings was the art and skill of asking myself the right questions. Successful self-interrogation can be a painful confrontation with the avoidance and denial that cloak our co-dependency. Nevertheless, self-honesty and accepting self-responsibility are absolutely essential to anyone who hopes to break through the injunctions that bar the way to an autonomous life.

Questions And Answers

The story goes that on her deathbed Gertrude Stein was asked, "What is the answer?"

Her reply was, "What is the question?"

That's something to think about for all of us who feel the need to change our life directions. Having spent our lifetimes looking to others for the answers to our problems, we've never learned to ask the right questions.

In pursuit of the easiest, fastest way to get what we want out of life, we often mistakenly go along with the crowd. We don't realize this is not the way to find autonomy. Autonomy is available to any of us willing to look deeply into ourselves and ask the tough questions that go with our quest for individuality.

Some questions you might ask yourself are:

- What's the central problem in my life right now?
- How do I feel about that?
- If I don't like these feelings, am I willing to change?
- How would I rather feel instead of the way I'm feeling now?
- How will I feel in five years if I don't do anything about my co-dependency?
- How will I feel about myself in five years if I become a more self-dependent person?
- What am I willing to do now to get where I want to be in five years?
- When am I willing to begin those changes?
- If I had the power of magic, what would I change about me in order to enjoy life and my relations with others?

Whether on your own or with the help of a professional guide, asking questions like these will help you get started on the road of personal growth. It may take some persistence and patience to find your answers but doing so will provide a firm foundation for moving forward.

Without asking such questions of yourself, you remain subject to the co-dependency you are trying to escape. With such questions answered, you can decide for yourself what to take and what to turn aside in the way of advice and counsel from others. Ask the right questions of yourself and you'll find the right answers to becoming an autonomous, self-actualizing person.

Self-Made Redecisions

As you go through the day, pay attention to the circumstances that trigger bad feelings for you. Are these feelings familiar?

Do they go on over and over in the same circumstances? Do you consistently suffer bad feelings when interacting with certain kinds of people?

For example, in communications training workshops a frequent complaint is "I *always* have a hassle with my boss when he orders me around." Or, "When my boss criticizes me I *always* freeze up inside."

In almost all cases, people making these comments are able to trace their feelings back to childhood experiences. They are also able to acknowledge that their current bad feelings are just like the ones they had as children. In adulthood they still have habitual "childlike" feeling-reactions when current situations appear similar to key childhood events.

You can check this out for yourself. Fill in the blank spaces of the following sentences:

Whenever this (describe the situation) happens, I *always* feel (describe the feeling that goes on over and over in this situation). _____

_____

Whenever I try to talk with (name of the person involved) I *always* end up feeling (describe the feeling you get over and over when interacting with this person or others like him or her).

_____

_____

Let's say, for example, you have difficulty asserting yourself in your communications with others, a rather common condition for co-dependents. Think about the last time you felt angry or resentful when you went along with someone else's program even though you really didn't want to. When was the last time that happened to you? And the time before that? How many times did it happen last year? _____

_____

_____

Did you have similar feelings in similar situations in college? In high school? In grade school? How was it in your family when you were small? _____

Did you have trouble speaking up to either of your parents or any of your siblings? _____

_____

_____

Some people have difficulty believing that their feelings as an adult can be the same as the ones they had as a child. If that applies to you, tracing your feeling patterns back to childhood may help you recognize the extent to which childlike feeling habits are negatively affecting your current affairs.

Most important, understanding the origin of your feeling habits will help surface the "Don'ts" embedded in your childhood programming.

Let's look at Suzy's history. She reports, "I never could talk back to my father. He just went berserk when any of us spoke up." That went on over and over in childhood with Suzy. As an adult she could never "talk back" to a supervisor or almost any other male, even if he told her, "Now look, I don't want any people-pleasers around here. It's your job to tell me if I'm wrong."

Some injunctions that go with Suzy's feelings are "Don't talk," "Don't make waves," "Don't speak up," or just plain "Don't!"

I knew an IBM salesman who gave up a promising career because he couldn't handle the objections of clients. When he had to deal with a prospect's resistance, he felt as if his answers were arguments. And his injunction was "Don't argue with me." He quit to become a teacher but didn't really like that either because all discussions were arguments to him and he couldn't handle the bad feelings that came with them. He let his past dominate his present and diminish his future.

As you go along with the process of tracking down the origins of your bad feeling-habits, you may find that your bad feelings of the moment will be dispelled as you do something constructive for yourself in the here and now. You will be engaging in positive instead of negative thinking — positive thinking attached to an inner reality that is true for you.

It is also possible that in milder cases of co-dependency, this process may lead to a self-made redecision. For some people the sheer power of logic will bring them in time to the point where they say to themselves, "I'm no longer willing to let what happened in my childhood continue to mess up my feelings and my relationships with others."

The promise to free yourself from the past is a turning point at which the process of self-made redecisions begin. Some people do this consciously and plan a new way to live their lives. Others do it unconsciously and grow into a new pattern of attitudes and actions that contribute to their increased well-being.

A Step At A Time

A guided redecision made with a skilled therapist can happen very quickly. In 20 or 30 minutes a person can go back in memory to childhood, recognize dysfunctional experiences and identify the feelings that went with them. By doing that you can uncover and then redecide the childhood decisions underlying the formation of habitual thinking-feeling-acting patterns.

Reprogrammed redecisions, the ones we make on our own, are a different matter. Self-made redecisions take a little more time and a lot more patience — qualities in short supply among those of us in recovery. Having believed for years that in some Cinderella fashion fate would rescue us from our troubled lives, it is difficult to accept the fact that we can rescue ourselves by redeciding our attitudes and actions "a step at a time."

As you move toward autonomy there are bound to be times when impatience gnaws at you or your Inner Saboteur floods your mind with negative thinking. When that happens, be encouraged by these words of Bob and Mary Goulding:

> Again, *redecision* is a beginning. There is no magic. The person discovers his ability to be autonomous and experiences his new, free self with enthusiasm, excitement and energy. He goes out into his world to practice changing and the changing is a continuous process. He looks upon the world through a different pair of glasses, a different pair of eyes, not coloring the world muddy and tainted by his original decision, but seeing clearly, sharply, as if the rain had washed away the smog. (4)

If I have one rule to pass on to others seeking autonomy it is, "Keep on keeping on." You'll be on the recovery trip a long time and many steps involve risks, facing the fear of change and moving through it. But every step is worth it. Take faith from the experience of the many who have gone the way of redecision before you. Believe in your heart that the passages get less rough as you go along. They do!

7

On Becoming Functional

My true identity is beyond anything outside of me.

— **John Bradshaw**

Getting functional is an inside job. It's a matter of discovering what works for you from the inside out.

How functional you are can only be measured by your ability to achieve the goals you have set for yourself. It doesn't matter whether your goal is to be the best shoemaker in town or to increase your peace of mind.

Eric Berne defined a Winner as "someone who accomplishes his declared purpose." (1) With your purpose declared you can get on with it. Winners do what is appropriate for winning. Losers compulsively do what is appropriate for losing. Co-dependency is a losing way of being in the world.

Twenty years ago, not knowing what it meant to be true to myself, my goals in life were in conflict with my desire for inner peace. Unclear on what I needed to do or not do in my search for greater self-esteem and well-being, I had no idea what was functional or dysfunctional. I didn't know how to become a whole person. Without any of the information about co-dependency that exists today, I had to wade through human-istic psychology, looking for whatever might be helpful to me.

Once having settled on autonomy as a good goal, my next questions were, "What is life like for an autonomous person? What are life's payoffs for an autonomous person?" In addition to Eric Berne's ideas on autonomy and Winners, I found two other investigators of the human condition whose concepts seemed right for me: Abraham Maslow and Gail Sheehy.

Maslow's Self-Actualizers

Early in his career as a psychologist Abraham Maslow noted that certain people he considered "fully-mature" had certain common characteristics. Excited by the idea that there were special people who enjoyed high levels of mental wellness, he called them "self-actualized." He said self-actualizing was "the full use and exploitation of talent, capacities, potentialities." (2)

Maslow's terms self-actualization, self-realization and self-fulfillment all reinforced my growing conviction that my well-being was my own responsibility. I was ready to strive for autonomy and authenticity.

Sheehy's Pathfinders

Gail Sheehy describes Pathfinders as people who have attained high well-being and have successfully navigated the various developmental stages of adulthood. She defines those periods of transition from one life cycle to another as passages. We move past certain recognized turning points as we grow toward higher levels of well-being.

Some of these turning points are "life accidents" such as the death of a friend or family member, divorce or economic disaster that dramatically influence the pace and direction of adult development. Other turning points mark the beginning and end of various developmental periods in the course of a human life. They mark the milestones along the path toward emotional maturity. (3)

Though Sheehy did not target co-dependency, it seems safe to include crossing over from dysfunctional living to functional living as a major passage in the life of a co-dependent. As with all passages, it is nice to know something abut the rewards of crossing over to that unknown territory on the far shore. Sheehy provided me with a picture of that territory.

I found Sheehy's 10 hallmarks of well-being a target of hope that what had been done by others I could do for myself. I had always resisted establishing criteria for my life performance based on a single expert's opinion about human behavior. However, Sheehy had arrived at her conclusions after reviewing responses to some 60,000 life history questionnaires. That was a big enough sampling of other people's well-being for me to have some faith in the validity of her research. I felt safe in using her hallmarks of well-being as goals to shoot for in my own search.

Sheehy's 10 Hallmarks Of Well-Being

1. My life has meaning and direction.
2. I have experienced one or more important transitions in my adult years, and I have handled those transitions in an unusual, personal or creative way.
3. I rarely feel cheated or disappointed by life.
4. I have already attained several of the long term goals that are important to me.
5. I am pleased with my personal growth and development.
6. I am in love; my partner and I love mutually.
7. I have many friends.
8. I am a cheerful person.
9. I am not thin-skinned or sensitive to criticism.
10. I have no major fears. (4)

There are three ways in which these hallmarks of well-being can be helpful to you right now:

1. On a scale of 1 (disagree) to 10 (agree) you can check out to some extent how your well-being stacks up against that of a Pathfinder.
2. You can use these hallmarks to help you define what well-being means to you and to set some guidelines for your own pathfinding.
3. You can begin to think about what you need to do that will be functional in moving toward a higher level of well-being than the one you now occupy.

Bradshaw And The Functional Human

John Bradshaw is an example of what it means to be a highly functional human being. He has used, is using and probably will go on using all of his vital force, experience and learning to advance the well-being of others and thereby advance his own. A recovering alcoholic and product of a dysfunctional family, he is well-known for his PBS TV series *Bradshaw On: The Family* and his bestselling books on shame and co-dependency.

At about the same time he was becoming a public figure in the field of co-dependency, I stumbled across some unpublished papers of his that include a few comments on the powers of being functional. My first thought then was, "Boy, If I'd known this 15 years ago, my way to recovery would have been a lot easier."

Bradshaw suggests:

> A fully functioning, vitalized, spontaneous human being has all his powers available to him: the power to know, the power to love, the power to feel, the power to be empathetic, the power to express, the power to imagine, the power to create. When all that works, you are functional. When it doesn't work, you're dysfunctional. That's as simple as I can make it. (5)

Though it looked easy enough on paper, I found this concept of personal power and human functioning harder to apply in real life. Not yet totally decided on goals appropriate to my intellectual, emotional and spiritual well-being, I didn't know what attitudes and actions might be functional or dysfunctional for me.

Now that many of my goals are realized, I have a better understanding of what it means to be functional and dysfunctional. I have a greater understanding of Bradshaw's ideas about the power to know, feel, love, empathize, express, imagine and create in the interests of my own well-being. What these powers have meant to me may help you choose for yourself what powers you need most to develop in order to become more functional.

The Power To Know

The power to know means much more to me than having the urge or drive to acquire knowledge of the world at large.

It means a power energized by the willingness to know your inner world.

This kind of knowing demands that we explore the dark side of ourselves as well as the bright side. It commits us to an on-going search for whatever feelings of worthlessness, evil, shame or weakness we manage to hide behind our masks.

To know yourself is to establish where you stand with yourself. Self-knowledge is the starting place for the long run toward self-actualization, authenticity and autonomy.

Give yourself some credit now for having begun that run. Believe in yourself and accept the reality that using your power to know is functional for your recovery.

The Power To Love

Feeling loved more for my doing than my being as a child, I found love a confusing word. My dictionary has 24 definitions of love. I've had to find out for myself what love means, how to express it and how I like others to demonstrate it to me.

My way of protecting myself from the emotional pain of being abandoned as a child was to close myself into a plastic shroud. I could see and be seen but no feelings went back and forth between me and those outside my shroud. When my father died I didn't cry and I felt there was something wrong with me. I did a lot of group work before I reached the point where I could believe anyone would ever really care for me.

Rowena says she grew up with a feeling of detachment. The chances for true intimacy between us were slight. We felt a kind of togetherness, but how much of that was love and how much mutual co-dependency we couldn't say. Now, after more than 50 years, we're glad something held us together long enough to enjoy our current state of contented companionship.

Three things you can do if you feel the power to love is lacking in your primary relationship are:

1. Be as accepting as you possibly can of your mate's individuality. Be willing for an equal state of OK-ness to exist between you.
2. Treat him or her as you would like to be treated. Show your love as well as tell it.

3. Open yourself to the belief that you are a lovable person.
   Learning to receive love is as important as learning to
   give it.

The Power To Feel

For some of us our "Don't Feel" injunctions literally crush our
power. We stuffed our childhood feelings down so deep we've
forgotten what it means to feel.

Even when we want to feel for others, many of us can only
intellectualize when a caring hug might be more expressive.
We've locked our feelings away in the closets of our minds.
Getting them out is the key to becoming a fully-functioning
human being.

However, getting them out of the closet is something to be
done with caution. A 12-Step group is usually not the place to
work on your feelings. The "no-crosstalk" rule stands between
you and any supportive interaction with the individual members
of the group.

The best way to work on your feelings is with someone who
knows how to be objective in helping you discover the origins of
your feelings and how to handle them. The best place to do it is
in a therapist's office or a therapy group. There you can learn
about and expose the deep-seated feelings of shame, rage, hate,
despair or hopelessness you've fought to conceal in the past.

Today the best use I can make of my power to feel is to let it
serve as an Inner Guide to whatever goes on within me. My
feelings work faster than my mind can translate them into
thoughts. Now that I know where they came from and what
they mean, I can trust them. I no longer struggle to stuff them
down. My feelings are a part of me and help to make me a
whole person.

Remember that as you deal with your feeling patterns, you
are lessening their power to contaminate your Adult ability to
make decisions and solve problems. One of the goals of therapy
is to get the garbage out of your feeling system so it doesn't
diminish your capacity to think for yourself.

The Power To Empathize

Empathy means different things to different people. The
meaning it has for me is best expressed by Everett L. Shostrom

in his book *Man, The Manipulator*. He speaks of empathy as a "charitable, altruistic love, which cares deeply for the other person as a unique human being." (6)

If you have too little empathy for others you could live a life barren of friendship and intimacy. If you have too much empathy you could live the life of a chameleon, constantly changing colors to match those you are with. Suffering from too much empathy has driven more than one nurse, minister, therapist or counselor from the helping professions.

Appropriate use of the power to empathize is to "walk a mile in your brother's shoes" without hurting your feet. It is being able to identify with others without losing your own identity in the process.

Without healthy boundaries or limits to our empathy we lose control of our lives. We surrender our autonomy to the myth that our well-being is totally dependent on doing more for others. Our identity is sacrificed on the altars of submissiveness and people-pleasing.

If you have difficulty empathizing, use your CoDA group as a place to test your sensitivity to others. There you can pay attention to your feelings. Which stories trigger your compassion? Which ones irritate or bore you? Does one type of person trigger your empathy more than another? Do you ever get the feeling toward another of that "charitable, altruistic love" spoken of by Shostrom?

Though you can learn a lot about yourself just through heightened awareness of your empathy responses in a CoDA meeting, you can accomplish much more in an encounter or sensitivity training group. You can check out with others how they feel and find out if your empathy for them is consistent with their response. Sometimes we can become so fixed in our view of others we defend our position in a way that stifles our power to empathize.

A few of us in our grandiosity confuse pity with empathy. That was certainly true for me. This was my "I'm OK — They're not so hot" position which covered up my own self-pity.

You can increase your power to empathize by active listening. You can give feedback: "It seems to me you're feeling sad." "Gosh, that must have made you angry." "I guess it's pretty awful to be breaking up like that?"

Then carefully listen to their response. Take their word for it that they are feeling what they say they feel. Don't let judgmental reactions diminish your power to empathize. Feeling patterns are not universal. What triggers your feelings one way might not trigger another's feelings the same way.

However you go abut it, discovering the appropriate balance of empathy for you will enrich your relationships with others.

The Power To Express

To express yourself is to put your thoughts or feelings into words, body language or action.

The power to express yourself functionally to get the results you want is tied to the power of your co-dependent injunctions. The greater the power of your "Don'ts," the less is the power to express yourself.

However, as you move forward in recovery and increasingly free yourself from your co-dependent script, your power of expression will increase accordingly.

Two strategies that might help in this matter of self-expression are:

1. Make a simple statement of your feelings. For example, when feeling angry you might just open your hand, place it against your chest and as calmly as possible say, "I am feeling angry. Give me a moment to think." This is certainly better than shaking your clenched fist, and shouting, "You make me mad!"

An excellent strategy I've found for myself is to hold up my open right hand and say, "I'm confused. I'm not sure I know how I feel about that." This keeps me from running my mouth inappropriately and gives me time to get my mental and emotional responses on the same track.

2. Sending "I" messages is almost guaranteed to be more constructive in your relationships than sending accusatory "You" messages. Sending "I" messages tells you and the other person that you accept responsibility for your feelings. By dropping the "You" messages you also drop the blaming, thus making it possible to communicate your feelings more openly and honestly.

Sending "I" messages is a masterful technique for avoiding games like "You make me mad," or "If it weren't for you I wouldn't feel like this." Always remember that in most cases you are dealing with another co-dependent who may have just as much trouble with self-expression as you have.

However, don't push yourself too soon or too hard in the direction of self-expression training. First things first. Do your self-discovery work. Get familiar with your thinking/feeling habits. Get some idea of what it would be like to be more self-dependent.

No matter how you go about your recovery and personal growth, you will be moving toward an increased power of personal expression. To throw yourself too strenuously, too soon, into the effort to be more outgoing could be self-defeating. Recovery, therapy or self-development are not processes to be rushed beyond your readiness for change.

Walk on, and as you shrink your co-dependency, you will expand the power to express yourself.

The Power To Imagine

To imagine is to form a picture or concept in your mind that is not present in the external world. How well you use that power is crucial to your transition from low self-regard to high self-esteem.

You can use it to wallow in self-defeating, negative thinking. Or you can use it to engender optimistic and positive thinking. It is a matter of choice. You can think of yourself as a happy, functional person and see yourself as the self-actualizing person you are working to become.

In *The Magic Power Of Self-Image Psychology*, Maxwell Maltz writes, "The power of imaging is fantastic." (7) Maltz, a famed plastic surgeon, proposed that our self-image is the foundation of our personality and behavior and that improving our inner "face of personality" can lead to improvement in our personalities and behavior.

Many of us carry in our minds a picture of our "face of co-dependency" that diminishes our potential for autonomy. By using the power of imagination that picture can be changed to a "face of self-dependency."

So be bold and daring. Imagine yourself as a happy, successful, self-actualizing and self-dependent person. Imagination of this kind is called inspiration. If we have the courage to follow it up with action, it usually becomes a reality.

The Power To Create

Creativity encourages new and better ways of thinking and doing, helping us break the bonds of co-dependency. The power to create is the power to bring new ideas from within yourself. When you exercise your creativity you actualize your thoughts, feelings and experiences. Creativity is your ability to dip into the rich wellspring of your individual life.

To fantasize, dream, imagine or visualize yourself in your desired way of being in the world is the foundation for creative recovery. Create in your mind a vision of what happiness would be for you; start creating plans and actions to meet your goals.

Read about creativity. Read about creative people. Take a course on creative thinking or creative problem-solving. Translate your new information into positive action and you'll be on your way to the kind of life you want.

Do what you can to exercise your natural power to know, to love, to feel, to be empathetic, to express, to imagine and to create. Do that and you will be on your way to becoming what Bradshaw describes as "a fully functioning, vitalized, spontaneous human being."

And while you consider Bradshaw's suggestions about the powers of being functional, you might consider one more I have found tremendously important in my own search for well-being.

The Power Of Willingness

The power of willingness is the power of commitment, conviction and determination. All of us have that power available to us but sometimes we are afraid to use it. We forget that willingness is a choice. We reject hope. In our unwillingness we protect ourselves from the fear of disappointment, a fear born of the repeated broken promises that were made to us in childhood.

But you are not a child now. You have a new opportunity of choice. You can choose a willingness based on your own adult knowledge and experience and let go of the Victim games of helplessness and hopelessness you learned in childhood. In your recovery you've acquired new coping skills your parents never had. You can have hope that your willingness to change will lead you to a better life than the ones they endured.

If you are not a self-starter, accept the fact that you were born with the same potential for willingness as those who are. You are no different from the thousands of people who have changed and are changing on their own, in therapy or in 12-Step programs.

If your willingness is weak, here's an affirmation I've used for years that might get you moving on the path of change: "I am willing to accept all good things that come to me as I practice positive thought and positive action in all of my affairs."

Say this over and over until it becomes an automatic response, quelling your twinges of negativity. Visualize yourself as a happy, positive person. You can make your dreams come true if you are willing to do what others have done to successfully recover from their co-dependency.

In *Dare To Change* I wrote, "Potent people know who they are, what they want out of life, and how to go about getting it." (8) One of the ways they go about getting it is to be as functional as they can possibly be in all their thoughts and actions. You can be as potent and as functional as you would like to be once you exercise your power of willingness to get on with your escape from co-dependency.

8

You, Me
And Us

We need to take responsibility for communication. Let our words reflect high self-esteem and esteem for others. Be honest. Be direct. Be open. Be gentle and loving when that's appropriate. Be firm when the situation calls for firmness. Above all else be who we are and say what we need to say.

— **Melody Beattie**

When two people get together on anything beyond a casual basis, a third entity comes into being. Suddenly there's not just you and me, there's also us.

"Us" is the bonding agent that holds a relationship together for better or for worse. It is likely to be for worse when unmanaged co-dependency is a major ingredient in that bonding. As the blinding flame of early attraction dims, couples begin to see each other as they really are. When differences in scripts, belief systems and values emerge, the "us" becomes strained, conflict takes over and compatibility fades.

In the absence of an expressed understanding of who gives what to whom and does what for whom, a relationship operates on a mishmash of assumptions. It lacks a purpose. It tends to drift along like a rudderless ship with nothing but hope to help navigate the sea of conflict that is present in almost all human coupling.

Co-dependency And Conflict

Conflict is inevitable when two people from dysfunctional families come together in a relationship. Each person brings to that relationship the flawed intellectual/emotional/behavioral patterns they learned in childhood.

The human gyroscope inside makes every possible effort to keep co-dependents clinging to the status quo. Unless the "us" in a relationship is recognized and individual concessions made for the common good of "you and me and us," the potential for game-playing and conflict will probably always remain high.

Put two people-pleasers together and constant guessing games go on as each tries to outplease the other. Put a Persecutor with a people-pleaser and life is a constant round of One Upmanship. Put a Hero and a Heroine together and the battle is on to outshine the other.

Conflict is not an inherent part of relationships. Two recovering co-dependents who are willing to commit themselves to compatibility and respect for each other's autonomy open the way to a harmonious relationship. Give up conflict in favor of compatibility and your relationship cannot help but grow.

Co-dependency And Compatibility

Compatibility is the capacity for enjoying harmony with others. A compatible relationship calls for a delicate balance between satisfying individual needs and relationship needs. It calls for the willingness of two people to accept each other's individuality and also creatively resolve the differences between them.

To give up conflict and live in harmony with one another, people need to answer the question, "How can I be myself and also enjoy the emotional and sexual fulfillment that comes with a compatible relationship?"

Surprising as it might seem, not everyone wants that question answered. To do so might shatter their illusion of being right or perfect. The contemplation of self-responsibility is just too threatening for some people.

In a workshop for singles I asked a retired military officer with two failed marriages behind him, "Are you willing to change anything about you to improve your chances for a better relationship?"

"No way." His vocal tone implied there was something wrong with me for even asking. "I'll find myself a good woman."

That closed the matter for both of us. My assumption is that for him a "good woman" and severe co-dependency are synonymous.

As you consider changes you might have to make to create a healthy us, another question comes up: "What do *we* need to do to get what we want out of this relationship?" We start answering this question by clarifying our values.

Values Clarification

In the glaring lights of romance it is unlikely either person will say, "Maybe we ought to talk a little bit about values clarification." Nevertheless, once the bonding process has begun, so has the identification of individual values, the differences between "my" and "thy" values, and the ways those differences will be resolved.

The big differences between two partners are easily identifiable. These are usually cultural, racial, social and religious. When black marries white, poor marries rich or Jew marries Catholic, it is usually apparent that compromises will be necessary if the relationship is to survive.

Potential conflicts of personal values, the hand-me-downs of childhood programming, are less obvious. For example, having an equal voice in family decisions is a positive personal value but not one often experienced in dysfunctional relationships. Always having the last word in a discussion is a negative value but is common in co-dependent relationships. Freedom from sarcasm is a positive value but in my family sarcasm was taken as humor. It took many years for me to learn that many people, including my wife and children, did not think my sarcasm was funny.

Perhaps you've heard a couple agree, "Oh, we handle the big things okay. It's the little things that drive us up the wall." The "little things" represent our personal values and are often the focus of constant Win/Lose skirmishes with our mates. Without conscious awareness of what we are doing, we keep ourselves locked in a struggle for power as we tenaciously cling to values learned in childhood.

Having usually assumed as children that our family values were typical of all families, we thought of ourselves as "normal," even though we didn't know what normal was. As adults we continue to think the same way. We tend to discount as abnormal or wrong those who don't agree with us. We frequently overlook the possibility that a middle ground might exist between our strongly-held personal values and those held by our partners. Sometimes only the pain of combat or the threat of separation will drive us to the bargaining table. And, judging by the divorce statistics, sometimes that middle ground is never found.

Hopefully, your partner willingly joins you in the effort to establish relationship values that permit each of you to be yourself and at the same time enjoy the love and friendship of a healthy "us." However, if that willingness is not immediately apparent, don't give up hope. Sort out your own values. Decide as best you can which of your values are no more than habit, which ones are important to your current self-worth and which ones might be negotiated or given up in the interest of greater compatibility.

As you consider this middle ground, keep in mind your first duty is to yourself. It is one thing to negotiate something for something on an equal basis and quite another thing to abjectly surrender your autonomy just to have a relationship, regardless of quality. Your goal is to move away from co-dependency, not toward it.

Be as objective as you can as you consider the personal values that are important to you at this stage of your life. In TA terms, "Use your Adult." Decide for yourself what values are necessary for you to be comfortable in any relationship.

A common example of differing personal values concerns the issue of punctuality. Margaret grew up with an alcoholic father who was always late for everything . . . if he showed up at all. For her to be left waiting provokes a great fear of abandonment.

Her husband Roberto grew up in Venezuela. The rule of *manana* prevailed in all household affairs. Roberto thinks of time in terms of days rather than hours and minutes. When Margaret fusses about his tardiness, he shrugs his shoulders and laughs.

When Margaret clarifies her values on tardiness and punctuality, she balances her childhood memories against the reality of the present. She recognizes her childlike fears are damaging to her individual well-being and that nagging at Roberto is damaging their relationship. She accepts as facts that:

1. Roberto is not an alcoholic like her father and isn't some place having "one more for the road" as her father had done.
2. Roberto loves her and will not abandon her.
3. Roberto grew up in a culture that does not see punctuality as a mark of character.

Sorting out her values about tardiness helps Margaret be more autonomous and free herself from a part of her childhood programming. She recognizes her nagging as self-defeating behavior and gives it up. A reduction in anxiety permits her to calmly tell Roberto the fear and worry she suffers when his tardiness is inappropriate. Instead of questioning him about his late arrival, she calmly states:

"I was afraid the sun might go down before you got here. This shopping mall is a dangerous place after dark."

"I really wanted to have the roast just right for you last night but I had to leave it in the oven too long."

"I'm glad you called last night to tell me you'd be late. That's a crazy freeway out there and sometimes I worry about you."

Slowly Roberto recognizes the values conflict between them about time values and punctuality. He agrees to make a greater effort to be on time and to telephone to let her know if he is going to be late. He tells her, "I really didn't know you worried like that."

And that's the healthy way things can go when people in a relationship examine their personal and relationship values, agree to resolve them and then get on with positive action. Values clarification and conflict resolution are key components in establishing and maintaining a fulfilling relationship.

Conflict Resolution

The resolution of conflict on a friendly, ongoing basis is the foundation for an autonoumous relationship, one that operates as much as possible free and clear of negative influences from the past. An autonomous relationship reflects the willingness of two partners to cooperate in a joint venture dedicated to both individual and relationship growth. It is the opposite of the co-dependent connection in which two people are driven to stick together in satisfaction of their co-dependent scripts.

Three characteristics essential to an autonomous relationship are mutual acceptance, empathy and commitment:

Acceptance

Accepting the many differences that cannot help but exist between two partners is crucial in a relationship. However, inappropriate acceptance is hazardous to the health of a relationship.

Inappropriate acceptance is acceptance of the unacceptable. Physical abuse is unacceptable. To accept it is to cross over the line that separates love and co-dependency. But not all differentiations between love and co-dependency are that clear-cut.

Knowing what is acceptable and what it not from a partner is usually learned only by experience. Sometimes learning what is unacceptable comes too late to save a relationship. What has been an irritation can turn into a burning resentment that cuts so deep the wound can never heal.

Getting to know more about your own character and temperament, as well as your partner's, can help you identify your differences and lay the groundwork for acceptance, compromise and conflict resolution. And exploring your differences might lead to some pleasant discoveries about your similarities.

One way of making those discoveries is with the help of a marital or relationship counselor. Another is with the help of the exercises and text in *Please Understand Me* by David Keirsey and Marilyn Bates. They say: "People are different in fundamental ways. They *want* different things: they have different motives, purposes, aims, values, needs, drives, impulses, urges. Nothing is more fundamental than that. They *believe* differently: they think, cognize, conceptualize, perceive, understand, comprehend and cogitate differently." (1)

That's a formidable list of human differences, especially for those who naively believe that "love conquers all." The Myers-Briggs Type Indicator, the basis for Keirsey and Bates's opinions, has been used for years in industry, business, education and government. It can help many couples realize that their differences are natural and not just an expression of "contrariness and perversity."

The Myers-Briggs Type Indicator lists 16 personality types. Considering the years Rowena and I have been together and our knowledge of each other's life scripts, it was still amazing to me to discover the many differences in our individual temperaments through using this assessment.

For example, until we discovered our temperament types, I didn't understand why I had so much trouble "making sense" to Rowena. It simply didn't occur to me that we might have some inherent differences in the way we saw the world. Many times I thought she pretended not to understand me in order to have her way, an attitude that did little to expand our potential for a harmonious relationship.

We discovered through the exercises in *Please Understand Me* that I am a "thinking" type and she is a "feeling" type. I immediately translate any experience into words. Rowena translates her experience into pictures.

I look at a sunset over the ocean and a textbook description comes to mind. That's my left brain at work. She looks at a sunset and sees the white fringe of the surf, the expanse of the blue ocean behind it and the wispy, pinkish clouds nestling close to the setting sun. She doesn't evaluate it, comment on it or try to figure out how she'll paint it. Her right brain functioning simply accepts it as it is and trusts that when she wants to recall it, the scene will be available in the file cabinet in her mind.

Now, when we have difficulty seeing eye to eye, I draw a word picture for her by using examples to illustrate my meaning. When she wants to get something important across to me, she takes the time to organize her thoughts in words by writing them out. As I have learned to accept her need for something other than logic and rationality, I've noticed that the friction that once troubled us has diminished.

Greater understanding of your own temperament, character and values, as well as those of your partners, can open up the way to increased empathy and intimacy between you.

Mutual Empathy

Sometimes people are willing to be more empathetic but their own "frozen feelings" pattern makes them incapable of it. Some people may be capable of showing empathy but unwilling to exercise it. They are so stuck in their "I'm OK — You're not OK" position that any show of empathy would amount to a surrender of their ego defenses, which they consider just too dangerous.

The willingness of one person to be more sensitive to another can be motivated by the desire or need for love, friendship, acceptance, acknowledgment or more worldly needs such as winning recognition as a good supervisor or getting a raise in pay. Whatever the motivation for increased empathy, the *willingness* to exercise it is vital.

The *capacity* for increasing individual empathy is a different matter. The wish to be a mountain climber is quite different from having the capabilities required of a mountain climber. In co-dependent circles, the inability to empathize is labeled "psychic numbness," "frozen feelings," or "stuffed feelings." They are dysfunctional feeling patterns learned in childhood and continued in adulthood. Not having feelings makes it almost impossible to be sensitive to the feeling needs of others.

It's been over 60 years since a little puff of smoke over the small chapel at Forest Lawn signaled my father's departure for other realms. I still remember riding home and wondering why I didn't cry as others did when people in their families died. It wasn't because I was being a "little man" and holding back my grief. I didn't have grief. I didn't have any feelings at all.

As I grew up, I reinforced my frozen feelings by developing a macho script that demanded a man be a man and keep his feelings to himself. I could have an intellectual sympathy for others but I couldn't empathize with them. My own stuffed feelings and "I'm OK — They're not OK" position wouldn't let me.

Such patterns can be changed but the task is not easy. It takes a lot of hurt to motivate most co-dependents to change. Yet changing feeling habits is the key to recovery from co-dependency. Many of us recognize the need to be more sensitive to others' feelings only after years of suffering rejection for our insensitivity.

Sometimes it is almost heartrending to listen to men in workshops puzzling over failed relationships. They are so programmed for "doing" they simply can't comprehend why others complain about their inability or unwillingness to communicate feelings. They say they are willing to *do* things for their mates but they don't know how to *feel* for them.

On the other hand, I've also heard many men say, "God, I'd have done anything! If she'd only told me what she wanted!" These complaints speak directly to the heart of the problems brought on by the "Don't Talk" injunction that haunts the lives of so many co-dependents.

Perhaps you feel you are giving more empathy in your relationship than you are getting but you would still like to make that relationship work. Don't give up hope until you are satisfied you have done all you can reasonably do to encourage the growth of mutual empathy.

Start by checking out your own message-sending skills in order to improve the ways you transmit your feelings. Make statements rather than ask questions that too often provoke a "Yes, but . . . " reaction. Your goal is gentle confrontation. Be careful you are not in a Victim mood that would trigger games of "Poor Little Me" and "Uproar."

Simply state your position and remain silent. Say what you have to say and wait for the other person's response. If it is favorable, you can go on from there. If not, disengage as gracefully as you can. To expect an immediate resolution of such longstanding problems is rarely realistic. Accept the fact that at the moment your partner is not willing to pursue the matter of empathy.

Contracting For Empathy

Consider asking for an "empathy contract." One partner might agree to give up some insensitivity while the other gives up hurt feelings. The agreement can be written or verbal. The action to be taken by each is agreed upon and a trial period is specified.

For example, Suzy says to Sam, "I felt you got mad at me last week when I told you the dentist said Cissy needs braces."

Sam grunts, "Ugh."

Suzy doesn't point out that Sam's "Ugh" discounts the importance of the issue. She waits a moment and says, "I'm feeling discounted. I feel it's unfair to be angry at me just because I had to give you the bad news."

Sam says, "Damn dentists. Greedy. Three thousands bucks, I suppose."

"Something like that, but I'm not talking about the money." Suzy knows Sam grew up in a family dysfunctionalized by poverty. "I'm telling you I don't like to be dumped on for something that's not my fault."

Sams thinks a moment. He says, "Oh, I'm sorry. I know it's not your fault." He buries his head in the newspaper, just as his dad did when questions of money came up at home.

Suzy calmly pulls the paper away from him. "No. I don't want to be ignored like that." She feels some exasperation rising inside but keeps it out of her voice. "I want to be heard."

"Well, hell, honey. I *am* listening to you."

"I know you hear the words but you don't really *hear me* and I want to be heard. I don't like it when you 'anger' at me for things I can't help."

Sam, an aggressive boss at work but a passive husband at home, is puzzled. "Well, I don't mean to do that. What do you want me to do?"

"I'd like you to listen to me just like you listen to your employees. You don't get mad at them when they tell you something goes wrong."

Sam sits back in his chair. "That wouldn't be good employee relations."

Suzy laughs at Sam's puzzled look. "No, it wouldn't. But how about some good family relations? Maybe we could practice some management skills at home."

They talk about that for a while. Sam has been genuinely unaware of Suzy's hurt feelings. In his childhood nobody in his family ever talked about their feelings. He is sorry Suzy feels bad but doesn't know what to do about it. He expresses his worry about the budget and the cost for Cissy's braces.

Suzy is able to talk about what she perceives to be a lack of appreciation. They both agree to pay more attention to each other's needs, Suzy's need for more compatible communications and Sam's need for reassurance that he is a good provider and that they will find a way to pay for the braces. In the conversation Sam realizes his anger is not about the braces; it is his typical reaction to questions about money and how they threaten his self-image as a provider.

The empathy contract they arrive at is that when Suzy has to give Sam unexpected news about family expenses she first gives thought to some budget planning. She'll say, "The dryer has just about run its last load but I think I can keep it going 'til the refrigerator is paid for. Then we'll be able to get a new dryer."

Suzy's contribution is to be more empathetic to Sam's need for reassurance about money problems.

Sam agrees to give up some of his unwarranted anxiety about money matters and not dump on Suzy when she has to bring them to his attention. His contribution to the contract is to be more empathetic to Suzy's need for not being "angered" at. They agree they will immediately begin to show a little more understanding toward each other's needs. They also agree that in 90 days they will have another discussion about empathy to see what's working and fix what needs fixing.

In doing this Suzy and Sam further commit themselves to their relationship and strengthen the bond between them. You and your partner can do the same in time if you are willing to cooperate in developing greater empathy between you.

Commitment

The line between commitment by choice and commitment by co-dependency is fuzzy and confusing.

How we handle the differences between us determines the nature of our commitment. If I compulsively give up all of my idiosyncrasies, beliefs and values just to have a relationship with you, I am acting out a commitment of co-dependency. I am valuing the relationship far higher than my autonomy.

However, if I value both my autonomy and the intimacy and warmth of my relationship with you, I might decide that I value some of my traits and quirks less than I do the perceived benefits of our connection. I might choose to give up some of my quirks in favor of deeper intimacy. If I do that autonomously, without making myself angry or resentful, I am committing myself by choice.

No friend, parent, teacher, spouse, mentor, therapist or sage can guarantee that his or her advice will guarantee happiness for the "us" of our relationships. We must discover through time, experience, pain and joy how to choose whatever balance of autonomy and compromise makes our relationship strong.

Communication

Communication is the transmission of an idea or feeling from one person to another. It can be as direct as a military command or as flowery as a love poem. In either case its intent is to "get the message across."

In co-dependent relationships many of us fail to get our message heard, our boundaries respected or our feelings honored in our longing to communicate with our partners. We often avoid the risk of speaking up or being honest.

We hint at what we want because we are afraid to be assertive; we hope our partner will get the message. We avoid hearing what our partners have to say to us because we don't know how to respond. Lacking autonomy we let our "not-okay" feelings rob us of the power to declare our needs or respond appropriately to the perceived demands of others.

If our relationship stands high on our list of personal priorities it is up to us to improve our transactional skills to become more functional and effective in communicating with our partners. A good place to start is to examine the two separate skills involved in the human communication process: message-sending and message-receiving.

Message-Sending

Sending "straight messages" uncontaminated by emotion or bias calls for clarity of purpose and intention. The major barrier to straight message-sending is fear: fear of rejection, scorn, ridicule, criticism, being ignored, being put down or shamed. Remembering that such fears are mostly old feeling habits will help you to be more assertive when expressing your ideas or stating your needs.

Specificity

To be specific is to face your fears, move through them and be responsible for getting your idea across to others. Specificity is an expression of autonomy and honesty. It is also the beginning point for compromise and negotiations, the give-and-take so important to healthy relationships. Some examples of specificity are:

- What I need from you is . . .
- Are you willing to . . . ?
- What I am willing to do is . . .

These straight messages stop many of the guessing games that go on in co-dependent relationships. The indirect, ambiguous, manipulative communication patterns we learned from our families keep us from communicating honestly with our partners. It is scary at first to change these patterns, but you may find your partner applauding the opportunity to be free of the persistent confusion inherent in your communications.

Specificity is both a game-stopper and an invitation to greater intimacy. It demonstrates your willingness to trust your partner's reaction. At the same time it opens the way for your partner to be honest in communications with you.

Vocal Tones

Words, according to researcher Albert Mehrabian, only contribute seven percent of a spoken message. Vocal tones contribute 38 percent of the message; the other 55 percent is conveyed by facial expression (included for our pupose here under "body language"). (2)

You know how the vocal tones of others can trigger your anger, rebellion, fear, sadness, frustration or any number of unpleasant feelings. You probably also have occasionally found it difficult to grasp the meaning of a message because of vocal tones that don't match the words. Gruff vocal tones can distort a message of caring. A light-hearted tone can dilute the seriousness of an important message.

If you want your message received as you intended it, be aware of your vocal tones and have your tone match your intent. A giggle is not appropriate for an executive order. A raging, bear-like shout is not appropriate for a message of love.

It may surprise you to discover how much your vocal tones echo the way you learned to interact in your family of origin. Cissy's childlike, whiny tone is a reflection of her "Don't Grow Up" injunction. Brett's gruff tones are hand-me-downs from his macho military father. Mother told me many times, "Push your voice out." As a man I've inappropriately "pushed my voice out" many times when a tender tone might have been more fitting.

Listen to your voice when you communicate. Feel the vibrations in your body as you speak. Say "o-o-o-m" out loud a few times and feel the pulsations in your chest and throat. Make a

squeaky noise and feel the sharp-pitched tremors in your upper
mouth and nose.

If a partner or friend is willing to work with you in a joint
improvement venture use a tape recorder to record your voices.
Talk about what makes you feel glad, sad, mad or happy. Speak
sincerely and you might be amazed how swiftly you forget
about the presence of the tape recorder.

Set it aside then and replay it a week later, listening to the
range of vocal tones you used. Think about tones that may not
have been appropriate for your message. Discuss with your
partner how you reacted to one another's different vocal tones
and how they colored your interpretations of the messages.
Especially listen for Parent or Child tones. This exercise will
help both of you improve your communications.

In TA terms, the object is to clear inappropriate Parentlike
or Childlike vocal tones out of the messages you send in order
to avoid "hooking" the Parent or Child in the person you're
addressing. Certain vocal tones can automatically trigger a
childlike, rebellious response or an authoritarian, resistant response from others, even though your intent is serious Adult-
to-Adult communications.

This does not mean all earnest communications should be
carried on in a monotone. There are times when it is appropriate
to sound like a parent or express the playfulness of a child. But
matching your vocal tones to the intent of your message will
foster better communications with others.

Body Language

The next time you watch television, pay attention to the body
language of the actors on the screen. Consciously observe the
many gestures and physical expressions that influence your
responses to them. Notice what a smile, a clenched fist or an
outstretched arm does to add to or detract from their words.
Consider the effort actors make to be certain their body language agrees with their vocal tones and words.

However, in your interactions with your partner you are not
on stage. You want to come across to your partner as sincerely,
honestly and autonomously as you can. There are times when
you especially want to communicate deeply what is in your
heart or on your mind.

At such times don't let inappropriate body language sabotage your intentions. Avoid Persecutor gestures such as shaking your forefinger at another. They are "rubber bands" to the past, reminders of teachers and parents who once triggered fear, anger or resentment in a child.

A friendly hug may be welcome at times but can also be interpreted as a sexual overture or smothering. Watch a little boy as he pulls away from his mother when she hugs him instead of listening to what he wants to say. What appears to the world as a motherly gesture may be perceived by the child as an effort to control him. So be sure your hugs are appropriate for the person being hugged. There are times even in a close relationship when attempts at touching or hugging are not appropriate. An unwelcome hug can be damaging to real communication.

Some people hate being touched. I was one of those before I gave up my "Don't Be Close" injunction. I took it as an effort at control or manipulation and automatically pulled away from almost any touch except in sexual situations. People who have been physically or sexually abused as children frequently have difficulty accepting either touching or hugging.

Two good ways to learn how your body language affects communications with your partner are:

1. Ask. That's right. Just say, "How do you feel when I tap your chest like this to get my point across?" Be sure you are in a good place with yourself when you ask for honest feedback. If the response is less agreeable than you expected, do not give yourself bad feelings. A sure way to sabotage good feelings in a relationship is to ask for an honest response and then display hurt feelings or otherwise reject your partner's honest feedback.

2. Go to a communications group together and learn how body language influences the communications between you. A video therapy group can offer wonderful learning as you watch yourself in action with your partner. Make certain you choose a skilled therapist. Watching yourself interact with your partner can trigger powerful emotional responses in either of you. If that happens, you will want a therapist you can trust and a group that is supportive and nurturing.

The Art Of Listening

Once you have gained a better understanding of the dynamics of message-sending and have begun practicing some new skills, you've met half the challenge of becoming an effective communicator. The other half is learning to be a better listener or message-receiver.

Listening at the deepest level is the ultimate act of love. It is the ability to, as Carl Rogers put it, " . . . hear the words, the thoughts, the feeling tones, the personal meaning, even the meaning that is below the conscious intent of the speaker." (3)

That kind of deep listening is rare in any relationship, much less a co-dependent one. Many of us are so locked into our co-dependent scripts we lack sensitivity to other people's problems. Old thinking/feeling habits diminish our capacity to clearly hear the depth of meaning in the physical, verbal and emotional messages sent to us by our partners.

We can expand our capacity to fully hear the messages sent us by learning how to "clear" our Adult, how to decode the messages and how to separate facts from feelings. These terms will be explained as we go along.

Clearing

Clearing is a process for keeping yourself "centered" and letting go of habitual co-dependent thinking/feeling patterns. It calls for reminding yourself you are you and not a reflection of the Persecutor, Rescuer or Victim roles called for in your old script.

To be clear is to be autonomous; to be in charge of hearing what is said to you instead of what you want to hear or assume is being said. Clearing offers the chance to respond by choice rather than habit.

Begin to improve your listening skills by paying attention to the circumstances that trigger feelings of being uptight or shutting down with "frozen feelings." Are there times when you feel angry or resentful but don't know exactly why? How about the puzzling times when you might not understand your partner's message but you fear asking what is meant?

As people talk to you, work at sensing any tensions in your chest or back or tightening of your gut muscles. Notice the times your thoughts or feelings blur the message being sent and you feel confused. Pay particular attention to the times your thoughts drift away from the subject at hand.

Habitual inattention can signal many things. It can be a signal that you are with someone you believe you "ought" to be with, rather than really wanting to. It can be a reflection of your own low self-esteem and a fear of saying something "stupid."

In my case, feeling detached means I'm having an attack of the "better thans." It doesn't happen often these days but in the past feeling superior was my unconscious way of protecting myself from low self-esteem and shielding my scared little kid inside. Everything would go blank inside my mind. I had to act as if I was paying attention even though my inner turmoil kept me from understanding much of what was said to me.

As you become more in touch with your feelings, you will probably find these distractions have a pattern to them. In one of my groups, Claude said, "When I was selling, I *always* got uptight talking to clients I thought were smarter than I was." Delores said, "When people talk to me about spirituality, I *always* get uptight. My mind fogs up so bad I can't really hear what they are saying."

Discover for yourself what your partner says and does that reminds you of the past. Recognize that your ability to listen clearly is being affected more by your history than by the events at hand. Claude remembers that he often felt dumb in the presence of his professor-mother and just "tuned out" when she explained things to him. Delores remembers that when her priest frowned at her, she thought she was bad and wouldn't go to Heaven. Then she'd feel so sad she couldn't hear what he was saying.

After those discoveries both Claude and Delores found it easier to clear their minds and hear their partners when their listening efforts were sabotaged by internal stress. When Claude feels "dumb" or inferior in a discussion with his wife, he says to himself, "She is not my mother." This clearing statement permits him to let go of the past and hear his partner.

When Delores's recovering boyfriend frowns, she reminds herself the frown doesn't mean she is bad. With this awareness of the connections between the past and the present, both are able to give all of their attention to the situation at hand. With their Adult clear, they are able to concentrate their energy on listening and clearly hearing the messages being sent them.

You can find your own way of keeping yourself in the present and clearing your receiving apparatus. Many people use deep breathing to relax their minds and bodies in threatening situations.

You can relax both body and mind by pulling a few deep breaths down into the bottom of your belly while you let your belly and diaphragm muscles slacken. You will probably find in time, if you work at it, that your energy flow changes. With that change comes a mental and physical relaxation that opens the way to a clearer understanding of what is being said to you.

Learning to "clear" doesn't come overnight but it will come if you continue practicing your communication skills. Your mind will become more open to receiving current data without being contaminated by old negative feeling and thinking habits. And, as you become more clear in your listening you will also find it easier to decode the messages being sent you.

Decoding

We all have our own ways of encoding messages. The words we use, our vocal tones and our body language all come together in a special way that is unique to us. To "hear" messages, then, calls for more than an auditory awareness. It calls for an interpretation of vocal tones and the ability to read body language. It is up to you to "decode" the messages sent you if you want to clearly understand them.

There are people who nod their heads yes when they are telling you no. When asked how they are feeling, others will frown, droop their shoulders and reply. "Oh, fine. Just fine."

There are also people who always talk by indirection. Instead of saying "I'd like to stay home tonight, rather than going to a movie," a person who speaks indirectly might say: "I feel like I've been on the go every minute this week. Sometimes it's nice to just relax and save your money for something special, don't you think?" Perhaps you have walked away from similar conversations and later wondered, "What did she really mean by that?"

It's almost as though people who send indirect messages are challenging you to decode what they say. You may also feel that some people are unconsciously afraid you will really get their message. If you can recognize the clues for the kinds of expressions that complicate messages, you'll be well-armed to meet the challenge:

1. *Verbal Clues.* Be sure a word means the same thing to your partner as it does to you. "Bureau" means a place to put shorts

and socks to some people; to others it means a department of the government.

When clarity is important, check it out with your partner. Say something like, "When I say *bureau* I mean a dresser. What does it mean to you?" Many messages go misunderstood because of differing definitions. Over time you can build a glossary of terms that have the same meaning for each of you. As you do that, the task of verbal decoding will become easier.

2. *Vocal Clues.* Vocal tones don't always transmit the same emotion or meaning for everyone. The gruff tone you hear as anger may be no more than your partner's everyday tone of voice, a part of his male identity.

If a particular vocal tone consistently bothers you, look behind it. What childhood memories are connected to it? What childhood feelings stir you now when you hear it? Do you get the same feelings now when you hear the same tone of voice, even though the circumstances may be different?

If so, check things out with your partner. Do some active listening. Say "I feel I'm hearing anger in your voice." Stop there. Wait. Don't explain unless asked.

Be careful not to assume you know your partner's mood just from the tone of his voice. Even though he dearly loves you, the pain of a twisted back or some stress brought home from work might bring a grumpy tone to his voice that you could easily mistake for anger.

3. *Physical Clues.* Pay attention to your partner's body language. Scowling at you and shaking a finger is a sign of a Critical Parent state of mind. A smile, a hug and pat on the shoulder indicate a nurturing Parent at work.

A level head, quiet hands and a calm voice signal a desire to engage you in an Adult-to-Adult transaction. Delight, laughter and smiling expressions indicate the Natural Child may be at play.

Nose-thumbing, a flip of the finger or obscene gestures are measures of defiance coming from the Rebellious Child. Tears, quivering lips and downcast eyes reflect the Compliant or passively Co-dependent Child.

The body language of all message senders is meant, consciously or not, to influence the listener's response or reaction. Both sincere and manipulative body language are efforts to control the outcome of any communication.

Your duty to yourself as an autonomous communicator is to avoid childlike, automatic reactions to your partner's body language. Perhaps you felt shame when your mother frowned and waggled her forefinger. Perhaps you were frightened by your father scowling and shaking his fist. These reactions, continued in adulthood, interfere with autonomy and clear communications.

As a message-receiver who wants straight, Win/Win communications, it is up to you to know your stimulus-response patterns. You need to be aware of those physical signals from your partner that provoke co-dependent reactions on your part.

While a clenched fist may mean anger, it can also mean the person is feeling frustrated and closed off. The co-dependent looks at the clenched fist and automatically interprets it in a single way — the way it was experienced in the painful past. The more autonomous person either asks what it means or observes carefully to find out what it means *coming from this person at this time.*

With increasing awareness of your habitual responses you can begin to give up your reactive habits. You can choose how you want to respond to a message without being inappropriately influenced by your partner's body language.

Separating Facts And Feelings

Facts are facts. Feelings are something else: a state of consciousness reflecting an awareness, an emotion or a sentiment. Examples are: a feeling of inferiority, a feeling of happiness or a feeling of compassion. (4)

One fact about feelings is that they can distort the facts. If your partner looks angry and shouts in an angry tone, you will not hear his facts unless you "keep your cool" and filter the facts from his emotional delivery of the message. You can actively listen with statements like:

1. "Tell me more about that. I'd like to know what's behind your anger."
2. "I can't hear you when you talk to me like that. Give me a moment to think."
3. "I hear your anger. Would you give me those facts again to be sure I have them right?"

Another fact is that logic alone rarely resolves issues where feelings are involved. When expressing irrational feelings, someone's capacity for logic is diminished. Before you appeal to logic, deal with the feelings. Let the other person know that you "hear" and respect those feelings. For example, you'll build intimacy by responding, "I hear how angry you are about this." You'll create greater separation and intensify your partner's sense of frustration and anger by saying, "You're getting all upset over nothing. Be reasonable."

As your autonomy increases so will your ability to separate facts from feelings. And your contribution to the "us" in your relationship will rise accordingly. But that is something you'll never know until you take action and run the risk of honesty in your communications.

It's important to realize that it's not going to work flawlessly every time. However, don't let an occasional failure cause you to lose faith. As Janet Geringer Woititz writes in *Struggle For Intimacy*, "In the real world, being vulnerable sometimes has negative results and sometimes positive results. But it is the only route to intimacy." (5)

Rowena and I can certainly testify to that. After having been slapped in the face as a child for honestly asking for what she wanted, it is still difficult for Rowena to clearly state her needs. "But," she says, "things do work better when I get my courage up and ask for things straight out instead of hinting at them." I agree. And I work at hearing her and recognizing that she does not demand the perfection I felt was expected of me in childhood. The intimacy between us rises and falls almost in direct proportion to the amount of honesty we allow in our communications.

The Third Self

The *us* that grows between *you* and *me* is the product of love, friendship and companionship. Whatever you want to call it, it is the essence of togetherness and intimacy. And it thrives best in an atmosphere of open and honest communications.

That kind of atmosphere rarely prevails in a co-dependent relationship until we leave behind our dysfunctional communication habits and develop constructive ones. For most of us the road to a better life begins when we start thinking in terms of us — not just you and me. If you can give up co-dependency as the bonding agent in your relationship and replace it with direct and honest communication, you'll discover the pleasures of intimacy, security and trust that can only belong to a healthy *us*.

Do what you can to give up the anger, resentment and fear that is the garbage of co-dependency. Think of friendship as Muriel James and Louis Savary described it in their wonderful little book *Heart Of Friendship:* "Perhaps this way of talking about friendship provides the most fundamental insight of all — that friendship is a thing in itself, that is real, unique, and personal. It can be called a *third self*, a new reality distinct from the friends themselves." (5)

You can work on bringing that new reality into being by exercising autonomy and improving the communication skills so important to the health and growth of "us."

ᏫᏇ 9 ᏇᏫ

Reprogramming Yourself For Happier Living

We each have to learn how to recover on our own.

— **Pia Mellody**

Now it's time to get it all together, to move from the general to the specific. So far we've discussed co-dependent scripts, the self-defeating games played to reinforce them, the negative power of injunctions and the redecision process that opens the way to autonomy.

Now let's look at a step-by-step guide to autonomous living on a daily basis. Remember, it's only a guide. Pick, choose and use what seems right for you. Your experience will tell you what works and what doesn't as you go about updating your thinking/feeling/acting habits in favor of self-dependency.

Looking Ahead

It's important to know the difference between worrying about the future and planning for it. Worry is a foundation for anxiety and stress. Planning is a foundation for setting up guidelines to achieve your goals. Life/career planning breeds self-confidence and optimism, traits not common to co-dependency.

Your first step is to have some idea what's in it for you if you change from co-dependency to self-dependency. What's your payoff for giving up the status quo and moving into strange territory? What price will you pay if you don't confront the fear of change and move on with your recovery? And how will life be if you do change and start becoming your own person?

Defining Happiness

Set your sights and narrow your focus on what you want and what you have to do to get it. Happiness is only a wish until you make specific plans and define the steps you are willing to take to achieve it.

It is important to define happiness as you see it rather than on terms defined by other people. Only you can decide on the changes you need to make to gain the serenity so often discussed by people in recovery. Know from deep inside yourself what you are willing to do to satisfy your physical, emotional, economic and relationship needs.

Keep in mind that defining happiness or serenity is an open-ended proposition. The more you get, the more's available. Be prepared to expand your horizons as you go along. Your happiness will grow as you walk on toward higher levels of well-being.

Setting Goals

Recovery from co-dependency is a wonderful goal. It is also terribly vague and unspecific. When autonomy is your goal, specificity is essential. You have many skills to master on your way to autonomy and they can only be learned one at a time. Maybe the starting place for you is increased awareness of your injunctions. Or maybe the first step for you is to learn how to clear your mind through meditation.

Autonomy is your major goal in recovery. Your minor goals are the skills most needed for you to achieve your major goal. Get to know these skills and then start with the one that seems most natural for you before going on to the rest.

As you go forward bear in mind that there are four stages in the movement from where you are now to where you want to go: wishing, wanting, committing and doing.

Wishing

Wishing is how most of us start on the road to recovery. We know life isn't going right for us. Something is wrong and we *wish* life would change. We wish "they" would change or "things" would change. Sometimes we even wish "we" could change, but we either don't know how to or don't believe we can.

It is important to identify wishing as an essential step on your recovery path. "Wishing won't make it so" by itself, but planning and positive action "will make it so" if you choose to Walk On.

Wanting

You change from wishing to wanting when you add one ingredient — intentionality. Wanting implies you intend to take action. Wishes are only wishes until you begin believing you can make them come true through your actions. At that point your intention moves you along to the next step.

Commitment

Commitment to recovery is something more than an impulsive choice or a routine decision. It binds you to the cause of freedom from your childhood programming. It calls for a meeting of the heart and mind in a joint venture dedicated to your overall well-being. To commit yourself to change is to trust yourself to do what needs to be done in the interests of self-actualization and self-fulfillment.

Doing

Doing is an essential part of being. All our wishes, wants and intentions are little more than a con job until we follow them up with positive action. Once committed to autonomy we have to *do* autonomy. We have to *walk our talk.*

This does not mean our self-worth is wholly determined by achievement. But right thinking means little unless followed by right action. If we are to be true to ourselves it follows there must be a harmonic convergence of our being and our doing.

Pia Mellody says, "We each have to learn how to recover on our own." (1) Doing that calls for more than wishing, wanting and intending. It demands commitment and action.

Recovery begins when our willingness to change blossoms into plans for appropriate action and we start doing what we've planned.

Choosing Your Way Of Recovery

There are many roads to autonomy. Some people find it without knowing what they were looking for. Some people stumble on it as they tag along with other seekers. They start out following the crowd but somewhere along the way they find themselves walking a path of their own choosing. Without consciously reprogramming their belief systems, they eventually develop a new outlook on their way of being.

Rowena says, "I don't know if I can really explain it. I read some books, go to some meetings, and later, things just seem different for me." For her recovery is a happening instead of a planned procedure.

When Rowena comes across something that *clicks* for her, she works on giving up old habits and getting on with new actions. She lets her experience be the judge of what is right for her.

Many people aren't like Rowena, though. They are more impatient. They may suffer more from their co-dependency. They may not have her faith in a Higher Power to help them along the way. They have to find their own way, whatever that way may be. Getting started is more important than looking for a guarantee that you have found exactly the right path for you.

Whether you are a right-brain person who *senses* the way along or a left-brain person who needs to figure things out, there are some known steps that can help you on your way to autonomy. How you use them depends on both your current stage of recovery and what you feel will work best for you.

Injunction Awareness

Making the connection between your old injunctions and what goes on with you in the present gives you the opportunity to choose between your old script and your new way of being. When negative thoughts or feelings affect you, ask yourself, "What triggered this thought or feeling when I was a child?"

Be aware of the old family rules you were not supposed to defy. Identify the "Don't" that is keeping you from being yourself. For example, a "Don't Talk" injunction might have you feeling scared about expressing your opinion. Remind yourself, "That was then and this is now. I don't have to follow that injunction anymore."

If you keep at it, your awareness of your injunctions will become almost automatic. Awareness makes choice possible. Once that happens, other good things will follow:

1. Previously unidentifiable fears connected with comparatively mild injunctions may fade away. My salesman son lost his fear of calling on strangers once he'd connected his here and now fears with those of a small boy talking back to Big Daddy.

2. Awareness of moderate injunctions provides the chance to take preventive measures to avoid anxiety or tension. Next time you go into a situation that has troubled you in the past, think ahead. Do the deep breathing exercises or deep muscle relaxation exercises explained later in this chapter. This will help you keep focused in the here and now.

3. Some of us suffer from severe injunctions brought on by physical, emotional or intellectual abuse in childhood. Those of us with such memories will probably need a professional guide to uncover our injunctions. Once we know our injunctions we can remind ourselves that *then isn't now*. With that reminder we can immediately choose how we would rather feel in the present. We can let go of old fears and get on with positive thinking and positive action.

Though it may sound corny, I have a little trick that works for me when negative thoughts or feelings warn me of a "glitch" in my mental computer. In my mind I see myself as a little boy standing by a real father. In childhood Mother called me by my middle name, Whitney. Now, when tugged by some vague, undefinable anxiety, I imagine this tall father-figure stooping over to give me a pat on the head and saying, "There, there, little Whitney. Everything'll be okay." Silly, maybe, but it works for me.

As you become familiar with your injunctions, you can use a variety of means to help you alleviate their negative power over you.

Daily Forecasting

Every morning millions of people check out the weather for
the day. The clothes they wear, the leisure plans they make and
sometimes even the routes they take to work are determined by
the weather forecast.

The suggestion here is that you become your own "stress
forecaster," checking out your emotional weather for the day
ahead. Set your alarm ten minutes earlier. When you awaken
give your body a good stretch. Check out your mood. What
kind of thoughts are floating around in your head? Are you
feeling upbeat and kind of zippy or are the blahs hanging over
you like a cloud? Think about your plans for the day. What
tension-provoking interactions with your spouse, your boss,
your kids or your peers may be on your horizon?

Doing this will give you some idea about your people environment for the day. If you foresee any stressful situations out
there, pinpoint the injunction that lies behind your anticipated
stress.

For example, Samantha knows she *always* gets uptight if she
has to make a presentation to her boss at the ad agency. She's
reacting to the "Don't Be Important" injunction that diminishes
her self-esteem. In her family women weren't supposed to be
important. Her dad was sarcastic about women cluttering up
the workplace. The feeling memories about that sarcasm sometimes overwhelm her at the thought of "being somebody"
around the office. When that happens she takes another peek at
the performance evaluation filed in her desk drawer. Her mind
clears. She relaxes as she reads her boss's comment, "Doing
excellent work."

Harelson has a strong "Don't" injunction. Like a good co-
dependent his style is to listen to others, test the wind and
follow the leader. He hates to make decisions. But as company
treasurer, his role for the day is to dictate the departmental
budgets for the coming fiscal year. He knows Jackson, the sales
manager, will argue like hell in favor of more money for the
sales department. In anticipation of that conflict, Harelson feels
queasy before he even gets out of bed.

He is still affected by the meekness of his co-dependent civil
servant father. Dad always preached the virtues of job security
and pension plans. When there wasn't enough money to go
around in a family of six, Mother would say, "Things would be

a lot better for us if your dad had some get up and go." When she was upset with Harelson, she'd say, "You're just like your father."

On the days Harelson faces a staff meeting, he tells himself, "Then is then and now is now. I don't have to be a carbon copy of my father all my life."

Self-Generated Stress

For the most part, you are responsible for your unhealthy stress. It isn't the job so much that bugs you. It's you bugging yourself about the job. The same is true of traffic, the people in your life or most of the other factors that stand between you and a reasonable serenity.

Looking at the day ahead and forecasting stressful situations is the first step in stress-reduction. It is a preventive measure against the buildup that occurs if you ignore or deny responsibility for your stress. With target situations identified, you can plan a course of action or learn new skills to handle such situations.

Bill, for example, has a strong "Don't Think" injunction. His dad used to bellow at him, "What'sa matter, stupid? Why can't you ever get anything right? Why don't you learn to think for yourself?"

As a computer scientist Bill does think for himself. He does it well and gets paid well for it. When he has to think in public, though, he blocks. His Parent voice beats at him and he freezes. His Adult shuts down. Any hope of speaking out is beyond him.

He dreads the brainstorming sessions in his company when everybody engages in a freewheeling thinking session. After learning about his "Don't Think" injunction and how it messes up the programming in his human computer, Bill turns off his father's voice. He autonomously decides his own thinking is OK and he is OK. Now, though he may still feel some stress in the brainstorming sessions, he no longer goes through the hours of agony he once spent in anticipation of them.

Review for yourself the habitually stressful situations in your life. How much time do you spend worrying about what's going to happen or feeling guilty about what has already happened? How similar are these situations to the stress-provoking situations of your childhood?

Let go of your childhood thinking/feeling responses. Change your negative thinking to positive thinking. Do some deep-breathing exercises when your body indicates you are generating stress for yourself. Give up the co-dependent games you play with others. Develop skills and competency. Do these things and the self-generated stress in your life will gradually fade away.

Belly Breathing

One dysfunctional teaching hammered into some kids is "Stand up straight. Pull in your stomach. Stick your chest out. Breathe into your chest."

Sometimes this results in thoracic or chest breathing habits. Charles A. Garfield in *Peak Performance* suggests such breathing fosters a dominant left-brain associated with reasoning and analytical skills. Diaphragmatic or belly breathing, however, increases the oxygen supply in the bloodstream and enhances right-brain activity. (2)

Co-dependents often learn early in life how to shut down their breathing in fearful situations. In my own childhood I believed I'd be invisible if I kept quiet and didn't breathe. I hoped if I didn't move a muscle whatever was wrong about me or my behavior would disappear.

Timmen L. Cermak notes that co-dependents in treatment will sometimes click into their "survival mode." "Their facial expressions become fixed, they seem to gaze off into the distance, *their breathing becomes shallow.*" (3) (Author's emphasis). Dozens of times in my communications or management training workshops, I've seen adults under stress literally turn off their breathing apparatus. The rise and fall of their chests stop. They sit motionless until a lack of oxygen triggers a big gasp and a heave of the chest indicates they have come back to life.

Just as you can increase your mental awareness of your injunctions, so can you increase the physical awareness of your breathing. Belly breathing, pushing your diaphragm down and letting your lungs fill with air, is a way to keep yourself among the living when suffering a stress attack.

When under stress, let your belly relax. Let your diaphragm muscles hang loose. Pulling some air deep down into your lower cavities and adding to the supply of oxygen in your bloodstream will see you through a stress attack and add to your autonomy.

Be warned, though, that when you let your belly relax you may be reminded of a parental voice that says, "You look sloppy. Pull your stomach in."

It was quite an exercise in autonomy for me when I first started belly breathing. It took some time to clear my mind of the many "Chin up, chest out, suck in your stomach" messages I'd learned in childhood.

One beauty of belly breathing exercises is that you can do them unnoticed by all except the trained observer. You can constructively deal with your tension without advertising it to the world. And the same is true of deep muscle relaxation exercises.

Deep Muscle Relaxation

Deep muscle relaxation is a "quickie" relaxation exercise adapted from Edmund Jacobsen's method of progressive relaxation. Jacobsen believed "an anxious mind cannot exist within a relaxed body." (4)

Clearing the mind of its troubles can relax the body and freeing the body from tension can promote peace of mind. However, sometimes the mind is so occupied with the business of living that we can't focus on clearing it. Muscular tension or queasy feelings in the stomach may signal us that we are troubled but we can't take time to sort out what's causing it.

We need relief fast. Deep muscle relaxation provides emergency treatment for muscular tension triggered by fears of disapproval, rejection or failure. The first step in this form of relaxation is to become more aware of the sensory differences between tension and relaxation.

Put either forearm on a desk or table. Make a fist and hold it tight. Be aware of the sensations in your hand and forearm. Now quickly snap your hand open. Let it relax. Notice how different the muscles of your hand and forearm feel. Do the exercise several times.

The glowing or flushed feeling you get in the muscles of your hand and forearm is the feeling of relaxation. If you do not get that feeling, move on to other muscles, perhaps thighs or buttocks, and go on with the exercise. Grip and relax. Grip and relax. You can go all the way through your body from the tips of your toes to your head. (Don't forget facial and scalp muscles.) Go ahead. Try it. If it doesn't immediately work for you, keep on trying. Tense up each muscle group just enough to allow you to see you truly can control how much tension or relaxation you carry in your body.

I've taught this exercise to hundreds of people in classes and workshops and most of them found the relief of progressive relaxation in a few minutes. It is an exercise you can do seated at your desk at work or even while waiting in line at the supermarket. In times of extreme tension, you might go into a restroom stall and go through the exercises for five minutes. At one hospital where I taught this, the nurses called it "the peaceful potty pause."

However, not all people learn progressive relaxation easily. If you need more help, read Charles Garfield's *Peak Performance* and work on the exercise suggested in his chapter on "Voluntary Relaxation."

Be patient. Teaching your body new habits requires practice and patience. The rewards are worth the investment of time and energy. In time you will be able to let yourself "hang loose." The feeling of physical relaxation that comes will help you untangle the troubled thoughts that brought on your tension. When tension strikes, a few minutes of progressive relaxation will help clear your mind and heighten your awareness of those Parent-Child dialogues in your mind that foster anxieties and fears.

Clearing Your Mind

Your first step toward reprogramming for an autonomus future is to clear your Adult. To develop new, more positive thinking habits, you'll want to cleanse your mind of its habitual churning, negative thoughts.

Brief meditation can rapidly clear your mind when under pressure. Meditation is a way of not-thinking, of allowing your mind to take a recess. To not-think is to clear the Adult of the old thinking patterns that interfere with the capacity to solve problems, make decisions or develop new thinking habits.

The next time your mind is filled with worrisome thoughts, try counting backward from ten to one. Picture the numbers in your mind or picture objects — ten apples, nine apples, etc. If troubled thoughts interrupt your counting, just let them go. Don't latch onto them by getting into internal debates. Pick up your count and continue. If you haven't reached control of your thoughts by the time you reach one, repeat the exercise.

Your concentration on counting or mental imagery will fill the space in your mind that has been taken up by negative thoughts. When you stop counting you have two options. You can choose to go on with the internal hassle that has been troubling you or you can choose to think thoughts consistent with being autonomous and authentic.

This may sound complicated but it is easier to do than to say. Do it. See how it works for you. If you have difficulty, keep at it until it gets easy. Give it a reasonable trial, say 30 days or so. If it doesn't seem to work for you by then, don't worry about it. You will have at least learned about the skill. What may not seem right for you today may seem right somewhere down the line.

Keep in mind that not clearing the mind when under stress is a form of self-sabotage. It is a way of hanging on to old, negative thinking habits instead of getting on with becoming autonomous.

Betsy, for example, feared her husband would leave her if she insisted on an equal relationship. She worried about getting a job and supporting herself and the kids. She kept her mind so busy with negative thoughts that she said, "I just can't think straight." When asked, "Do you mean you *won't* think straight?" her response was a blank stare. Her "Don't Think" injunction kept her locked into her self-defeating outlook on life rather than taking charge of her thought process.

After learning how to clear her mind with belly breathing, deep muscle relaxation or brief meditation, Betsy started plugging into her Adult. She decided to consult a marriage counselor who helped her get her ideas across to her husband.

Whatever means you use to clear your mind of anxiety and apprehension marks a starting point for autonomous thinking. It opens the co-dependent mind to its potential for functional thinking and grants relief from your self-generated stress.

Reprogramming

Reprogramming is somewhat like hitting the delete key on the keyboard of a word processor. Suddenly a line, sentence or paragraph is wiped off the screen and space is left for new information.

The difference, though, between computer programming and human programming is that human software has a life of its own. Original decisions, injunctions and childhood thinking/ feeling patterns are etched in. It takes a lot of time, perseverance and patience to wipe out old dysfunctional self-perceptions and reprogram ourselves as happily functional human beings.

Keep in mind that it took a good part of your life to become the person you are. Your co-dependency was learned bit by bit, day by day, for years. It can be unlearned the same way, using several different tools.

Positive Affirmations

Positive affirmations "kill two birds with one stone." The moment you think or speak the first words of a positive affirmation you introduce an antidote for the negative poison running loose in your mind. At the same time you also exercise your natural right to choose the direction of your thoughts.

Positive affirmations are not simply platitudes, repeated over and over. They are an exercise in active thinking. They deal in specifics, not generalities. They affirm your willingness to take specific actions that promote your autonomy. Here are some examples:

"I am asserting myself with my husband in the honest expression of my needs."

"I am competently writing the advertising copy my boss expects of me."

"I am being straight and honest with everyone I talk to today."

Affirming yourself in this manner reinforces your right to think for yourself. It is functional thinking by choice as you replace your old "not OK" thoughts about yourself with positive ones. It is an indication of your willingness to be the master of your mind.

Positive affirming reinforces your decision to be the person you choose to be rather than the co-dependency person you have been in the past.

Mental Rehearsals

While positive affirmations replace negative thinking, mental rehearsal provides you with a plan to put your new positivity into action. In your mind's eye you see yourself taking competent action to meet your goal as an autonomous human being, just as top athletes program themselves for winning a gold medal.

You can do all this as you go about your daily activities, making choices between co-dependency and autonomy. Having set a reasonable goal for yourself and reinforcing it with a positive affirmation, picture yourself doing it.

Let's assume for the moment that you have trouble with a "Don't Speak Up" injunction and it is agonizing for you to present your views to a group. You might affirm to yourself, "Today I am competently and confidently presenting my views at the staff meeting." Then in your mind's eye, see yourself standing at the blackboard in your meeting room. With a pointer you are emphasizing the facts outlined there. You are responding directly to questions with the facts you have so carefully researched and organized. As you leave the room, you hear someone say, "Well done!"

Don't confuse mental rehearsal with wishing or daydreaming. Mental rehearsal has the energy of commitment in it. Remember you have made a new decision to be free of your old co-dependent script. See yourself as a Winner, do what Winners do and one day you will be a Winner.

In our first attempts at mental rehearsal some of us have difficulty creating pictures in our minds. This was true for me. Then one day my friend Ed, who has taught mental imagery techniques to hundreds of counselors and therapists, said, "Don't worry about it. Tell yourself you are seeing it and in time the imagery will come." He was right. So if you find it hard to get a picture in your mind, just tell yourself you are seeing yourself engaged in specific self-actualizing activities. For many people the mental picture is simply an *impression* of themselves doing something they wish to do; it need not be a picture exactly like you would see on television.

Positive Pictorializing

Positive pictorializing is a reinforcement of your efforts to create in your mind a new image of you. It is a visual reminder

that you are on the path of recovery and are moving toward
new goals in life.

In my workshops we always enjoy ourselves making a "success collage." We sit around and thumb through a big heap of
old magazines on the floor. We look for pictures of someone
who appears to be living the life we'd like to live or who resem-
bles the kind of person we'd like to be.

We cut out four or five pictures that appeal to us, paste them
on cardboard and take the collage home to hang in a place
where we can see it regularly. The collages serve as gentle
reminders of our redecisions and our determination to make
successful changes in ourselves.

Will a collage help you reprogram your concept of you and
your achievements in life? Many people have found it gives
them inspiration. It pulls them forward toward a more positive
future. But you also must *act* to make your dreams come true.
Your imagination doesn't know the difference between its vi-
sions and reality. It accepts as truth what you feed into it.

Rowena and I did our collages many years ago and today we
live the life we pictured then. She hasn't ridden a motorcycle yet
but on her sixtieth birthday she did learn to water ski. We have
the place in the country we envisioned. She paints, I write and
every day the weather permits we walk on the nearby beach. All
these were part of those early collages we made for ourselves.

If you make a positive picture of yourself in your mind, plan
accordingly and take positive action to fulfill your plans, your
mind will gradually accept that what it sees is true. One day in
the future you will wake up with a new positive regard for
yourself. Match that positive regard with positive action and
you can literally create a miracle in your life.

Positive Doing

One more time. *Do it!* Do what is appropriate to your recovery from co-dependency. How do you find out what is appropriate? By observing others who are autonomous, getting feedback
from a competent professional or by taking risks and experiencing life.

Continue whatever you are doing now to escape from co-
dependency. Read all you can about how others are handling
their recovery. Go to groups. Listen. Think. Don't impulsively

rush out and do everything you hear others do, but be willing to take risks fitting to your recovery. Do what makes sense to you and feels right for you.

Autonomy is as autonomy does. Sure, you'll be scared and even hurt sometimes, but Walk On. Autonomy never finds anyone who is hiding in the closet.

Positive Predicting

For years I let circumstances predict how my day would go. I let myself be victimized by the external forces of my environment. I reacted to life rather than choosing it. Then I began to learn to predict how I would make my life go, followed by doing what I could to live up to my predictions. Positive predicting on a daily basis helps me foretell where, when and with whom any negative dynamics might creep into my day.

When you wake up in the morning lie still a moment and get a feeling for what is going on in your body. Your energy level will determine to some extent how you live up to your predictions for the day.

Take a few deep breaths — belly breathing. Tense and relax your body several times. Feel the energy stirring within you. Now think about the day ahead. Who do you have to talk to that might present a problem for you? What do you have to do that might trigger feelings of failure or rejection? What troubling "Don'ts" do you face ahead? What can you do to avoid self-sabotage in the day ahead?

Do positive affirmations about whatever difficulties you spot. Say out loud or to yourself, "I am calmly and confidently outlining our new company policy." Then do a future projection and see yourself doing it. Mentally rehearse, seeing yourself doing it. Envision yourself living the good life that goes with freedom from co-dependency.

Do that day after day, and sooner than you think you will be living the life you want for yourself.

The Reprogramming Package

Let me repeat. Repetition is the key for successfully reprogramming yourself from co-dependency to autonomy. Taking self-actualizing action over and over is the stairway to a happier, more fulfilling life. Updating a positive belief system on a daily basis is essential to developing a robust self-image and comfortable self-esteem.

There are bound to be times, especially in the earlier stages of your reprogramming, when old thinking/feeling habits will still push you into dysfunctional behavior. When that happens a handy pocket guide can help you get back on your chosen path. Write these five questions on a card: (The parenthetical comments needn't be written out. They are thought provokers.)

1. What's going on with me right now? (This question will help you focus on the here and now.)
2. How am I feeling about that? (Is this a repetition of feelings felt in childhood?)
3. How am I sabotaging myself? (What game am I playing or what injunction is influencing my thoughts, feelings and actions?)
4. How would I rather think, feel and act? (This is a reminder that you have the power to think, feel and act *as you choose.*)
5. What am I going to do about that? (It's up to you now. There are only two options. You can continue your dysfunctional attitudes and actions or you can give them up and learn new ones functional to a bright new way of living. It's your choice.)

Fold the card and put it in your purse or wallet. When your feelings disturb you or your thinking turns to the negative side, take out your card and review the items. It will serve as a conscious reminder that you are running your own show now.

Faith In Your Inner Power

Believe in yourself. Believe you have the natural right to be as successful and happy as you choose to be. Learn to trust the Inner Power generated by desire, will, spirit, tolerance and faith.

Desire

Desire is a motivator for change. Without the desire to be something more than what we are, few of us would ever change. The desire to be autonomous is the root of recovery from co-dependency.

Will

Will is a collective label for the forces of desire, motivation and self-determination that stimulate us to conscious action. It encompasses volition, the act of choosing and resolving to be the person we have decided to be. Will provides the psychic energy necessary to fulfill our chosen goals.

Spirit

The power of spirit is the power to function at the highest levels of physical and mental capacity. To infuse spirit in yourself and your outlook on life is to introduce increased vigor and vitality into your personality. To be high-spirited is to be characterized by enthusiasm, optimism and vivacity. It gives permission to feel good or be successful without having to later pay a price of shame or guilt for having defied the "Don'ts" in your belief system. Your spirit cannot help but expand as you move closer and closer to becoming a self-dependent person.

Tolerance

To be tolerant of yourself is to be accepting of yourself. To be tolerant of others is to accept them as they are without being sucked into co-dependency with them. Your tolerance of yourself will grow in direct proportion to your release of self-condemnation. Your tolerance of others will grow in direct proportion to your release of judgmentalism and your need to validate yourself by unhealthy people-pleasing.

Faith

Faith is a belief not necessarily based on probability. It is confidence or trust in a thing, a person or a concept. Faith is faith whether it be placed in God, Buddha or a piece of crystal from the Arkansas hills. Faith is something you can choose to have. To put trust in yourself is to put faith in your Inner

Power to guide you toward a path of goodness and well-being in your life.

Your Power Pack

Think of your Inner Power as a five-cell power pack. Its energy output depends on the care and maintenance of each cell: desire, will, spirit, tolerance and faith. When faith in your Inner Power runs low, as it is bound to from time to time, check out your goals, your commitment to them and your willingness to have good things happen in your life. Refresh and renew your belief in the faith that your Inner Power will keep you on your right path as you work your way toward peace of mind and harmonious relationships with others.

Enjoy

Put a little fun in your life. Don't forget the Child within you needs to play from time to time. Some of us didn't get the chance to do that in childhood. Survival took all of our energy, time and attention. So nurture yourself with a little *appropriate* pleasure along the way.

Go for a walk on the beach. Knit an afghan. Go surfing, fishing or skiing. Do what you want to do from time to time and forget those scolding Parent voices that shout, "Don't Have Fun."

It's your life now. Enjoy it.

❦ 10 ❧

Afterword:
Well-Being Report
On A Recovering Family

All of the ingredients in a family that count are changeable and correctable — individual self-worth, communication, system, and rules — at any point in time.

— **Virginia Satir**

Hope is available to all those willing to borrow from the experience of others. That's certainly true for Lynn, Whitney, Rowena and me. We hope you'll find it true for you.

Actually we are only four-fifths of the family. Our 47-year-old son is not included here because he does life the traditional way and does quite well at it, at home and at work. If he were to evaluate himself by Sheehy's Well-Being Scale, I'm sure he'd rank among the top five percent.

The other four of us might be called a living laboratory in individual and collective recovery from our childhoods. We are probably all older than many of you reading this book, but we see recovery as more a state of being than a chronological stage in life. We agree with Virginia Satir that family recovery can come about "at any point in time." (1)

Compared To What?

The assumption of this report on family recovery is that the well-being of a group is determined more or less by the well-being of the individuals in it. We see our collective well-being as a measurement of where each of us is in our individual recovery from co-dependency.

We arrived at this conclusion by using the Well-Being Scale developed by Gail Sheehy for her studies of the people she called Pathfinders. To simply state that the four of us now enjoy high levels of well-being invites the question, "Compared to what?" Our answer is, "Compared to the 60,000 people evaluated in Sheehy's research concerning people of high well-being."

We hope knowing a little about our life experience, the past degree of our co-dependency, and how we got to our current levels of well-being will encourage you to press ahead on your journey of recovery. Take assurance from the fact that each us knows how it feels to want to just give up and let life pass us by. And each in our own way knows that discouragement and hopelessness are only temporary barriers to those who are willing to Walk On.

The Silent One

Whitney, age 44, has been married to Tom for more than 20 years. Recently in the space of a single year she welcomed her retiring husband home from the Navy, released her eldest daughter to marriage and celebrated the birth of a grandson. She says, "And boy, there's a bundle of co-dependency issues in all of that stuff."

Along with all that, she's making nice progress in her late-blooming career as a vocational education teacher. At the same time she's taking night courses required for certification in her work. Like her mother, Whitney is an example of the married women who find their way out of co-dependency after their children become more self-sustaining.

Whitney can't say today why she chose silence as her coping strategy in childhood. She agrees her major injunction is "Don't speak up." She says, "I don't know why I was so scared all the time, but you were so big." I'm six feet four and when she was a child a high-crowned Stetson was part of my U.S. Border

Patrol uniform. I imagine I looked like a giant to her. She's also told me my strong voice scared her.

And she adds: "My brother and sister were so vocal I guess I decided speaking up took too much effort and guts. It was easier to play games of Stupid or Dumb."

At about age 28 Whitney grew tired of her timidity. When she and her husband were based in Japan, she was too afraid of life to venture out. But she developed new life skills and she changed. A few years later she was comfortably careening around in the insanity they call traffic in Honolulu, driving with the imperturbable confidence of a New York taxi driver. This is an example of how increased competency in life skills can contribute to self-worth and self-dependency.

Her first steps toward recovery began with some TA training. I talked about it all the time at that point. Her husband also used TA in his work as a Navy career counselor; but Whitney says, "He didn't apply it at home and that was frustrating."

As a Navy wife Whitney was able to get professional counseling to help with family problems when her husband was on sea duty up to a year at a time. In more recent years she has also attended ACoA and co-dependency groups from time to time.

Of her growth she says, "I don't know. I just did what it seemed like I had to do at the time. You know we never knew what co-dependency was until Lynn brought it up about four years ago."

Whitney feels an important part of her progress toward autonomy comes from her academic and career advancement. She says, "Getting ahead in my work gives me a sense of personal power I never had when I was younger."

On the Well-Being Scale she scores above average on 22 of the 24 items evaluated, ranking with exceptionally high well-being.

Of the future she says, "Hey, I'm not even 50 yet. I've got lots of good stuff ahead. And I've come a long way. Four years ago I'd have scored below average on 16 of the 24 items on the Well-Being Scale."

The Angry One

Lynn, age 43, is the youngest woman in the family and has paid the highest price of any of us for her co-dependency.

She was born mad and got angrier along the way. Now we know it's possible she felt unwelcome in the womb, but back in

1946 no one ever talked of prenatal programming. No one considered then that a mother's anger about an unexpected pregnancy might be transmitted in her bloodstream.

In her crib Lynn struggled so hard to turn over, she turned
blue in the face. She pushed us away when we tried to hold or
hug her. When she was three months old, we nicknamed her
Stormy. How were we to know this name would become a self-
fulfilling prophecy? In her early years she learned to hide her
anger behind a bright, sunny smile. Her childhood was filled
with resentments because she wasn't permitted to do the things
her older siblings did. She hated being the youngest child.

In high school she discovered that alcohol was an equalizer. It
gave her a feeling she had never had before of being equal to
others. After high school came an unwanted pregnancy, a short
and unfortunate marriage, and a 15-year life on the run with
dope and addictive love.

When she at last came home, all she had was a four-year-old
boy, a beatup old suitcase and the remnants of the bright, shiny
smile that had seen her through her childhood. She and her son
made a home of sorts in our double garage. She got help from
the Aid for Dependent Children program and went into a work-
training program.

They were stormy times but peace slowly came into her life.
Her violent mood cycles began to level out after she got free
from alcohol and drugs. That left her with sugar and co-dependency as the enemies of her tranquility.

When she kicked the sugar habit, 60 pounds and her addictive
husband went with it. She was finally free, at age 40, to begin
her recovery from co-dependency. Today she is employed as a
"corporate gofer." She's a receptionist, bookkeeper, service rep-
resentative and occasional truck driver. She calls herself a "professional co-dependent," meaning she chooses to more appropriately employ her co-dependent traits for the furtherance of
her career.

There are still times when her co-dependency bothers her,
but she's made great progress and now knows the joys and
rewards of being a whole person. She has the clear look about
her that I see in people who have "walked their talk" and have
done what they needed to do. She can be herself with me; a far
cry from the girl who told a school counselor, "I feel stupid
when I'm around my father."

Her way to recovery has been similar to the path taken by millions of people in 12-Step programs. She truly believes God loves her and means for her to go on getting better. She gives Heather Ture, her therapist, a lot of credit for helping her find her way out of co-dependency.

Lynn says, "It's like I never knew how I was supposed to be in the real world. When I check in with Heather, she hears me. I tell her how I've handled something and how I feel about it. She helps me get everything connected so I know when I've been functional or dysfunctional."

That kind of purposeful feedback has given Lynn her richest reward for all the struggles she's gone through in recovery. She says, "The greatest gift for me is to be able to trust myself to do what is right for me. Sure I make mistakes, especially with my son, but when that happens, I tell him I was wrong and we work things out."

Like Whitney, Lynn scores above average on 22 of the 24 items evaluated on the Well-Being Scale. And that's quite a distance she's traveled. Four years ago when she first heard of ACoA-ism and co-dependency, her score on the scale would have been way below average on at least 21 of the 24 items.

Of that scale Lynn says, "Hey, it feels good to know how you stand with all the other 'normies' in the world."

The Good Woman

Rowena is 75, has been married more than 52 years, is mother of three, grandmother of five and great-grandmother of one. She grew up in the days when "a good woman" stuck with her drinking husband and did what she could to rear her children.

As a girl she learned to live a life without hope, described in Chapter Four.

Rowena didn't set out to recover from co-dependency. That happened as she listened to the girls and me talk about it. She read some books, went to some meetings and became more competent in her painting. Slowly she has grown to the point where she can suggest what she wants or disagree with me without feeling angry. She grew bolder and bolder in expressing her thoughts about this book and finally began valuing her contribution to it as much as I do.

She's also steadily grown closer to her daughters as they've swapped the intimacies of their life histories. There's a lot of love

and laughter around the house these days when they get together. Rowena says, "The greatest thing that's happened to me in the
last four years is that I finally know what it means to feel hopeful.
I can begin a picture without predicting disaster. And I'm just
beginning to realize how we've made many of our dreams come
true." That dream was always a place of our own in the country
where we could do our own thing and let the rest of the world go
by. And we've got that now. It's a dream we've made real in spite
of a lot of struggle with addiction and co-dependency.

On The Well-Being Scale Rowena scores up with those
Sheehy rates as being of "especially high well-being." She agrees
with Lynn and Whitney that it feels pretty good to rank that
high after a lifetime of feeling so terribly "Not OK." Like the
girls, she's come up a lot from the below average rating she
would have given herself four years ago on the Well-Being Scale.

The Pretend Macho

I'm 74 and have the same marital and parenting credentials as
Rowena.

You've already read much of my life history in bits and pieces
throughout this book. One way to sum that up would be to say
that for 50 years I tried to do the "manly" thing without ever
knowing what it meant to be a male.

Nobody ever defined "man" for me. I went through life
guessing what it meant. I had to get through my "Don't Trust,"
"Don't Feel," and "Don't Be Close" injunctions before I could
enjoy the intimacy and self-esteem that comes with being an
autonomous male.

I thought I had done all my developmental work when Lynn
and Whitney first began talking about co-dependency. Over
the next four years, however, I discovered I had some unfinished business.

I had to say goodbye to my little girl Lynn and welcome the
adult woman, my friend Lynn. She was clean, sober and disen-
gaged from her love addiction but I still had the feeling I should
be her Rescuer. That's pretty much resolved now, partly because
we both made major moves toward autonomy.

The gain that has been the most rewarding for me in the last
four years has been a deeper understanding of Rowena and the
depths of her difficulties with her "Don't Be Yourself" and
"Don't Assert Yourself" injunctions. Listening to all three of the

women in my life talk about their formative years, their injunctions and their struggles to achieve personhood in a "man's world" has increased my sensitivity to all of them. And it has allowed us all to share a deeper intimacy.

But Rowena is the one to whom I owe the most. The only way I know to repay her for all she's given me is to be as kind and gentle as I can in making these winter years as bright and sunny for both of us as I can.

My rating on the Well-Being Scale is quite high, but I was surprised that only four years ago I would have scored below average on eight of the 24 items. My interest in co-dependency and helping others has taken the sting out of aging for me. At age 70 I began to suffer some self-pity, feeling cast off and ignored by the world of people busy "going places."

Those feelings are gone now. I'm back into teaching workshops and have dug up enough new material on human behavior to keep me writing books as long as I can get to my word processor. I've found my meaning and purpose in life and am at peace with my family. Those are things that create a natural high for me in these elder years.

Wisdom And Well-Being

Part of the wisdom of recovery is recognizing that our sense of well-being goes up and down and that's okay. A better job or a new relationship can be a real upper; losing a bid for a promotion or having a bad argument with a loved one can be real downers. And the ups and downs all challenge our well-being.

Perhaps one of the biggest discoveries we make in recovery is that how we feel inside does not depend wholly on what's happening outside. What we built inside us in the way of strengths, skills and self-dependency can allow us to meet every challenge and come out feeling a deep appreciation for ourselves. When the going gets rough, we needn't fall back on old co-dependent patterns that reduce our self-esteem and cause us to become fearful and defensive.

Tend to your inner and outer well-being and see your life as an exciting journey rather than some distant destination. You'll find, as we have, that the trip gets better all the time.

Appendix:
Walking On

There are many paths to take and many ways of walking on the road of recovery. Some walk their path alone, finding within themselves what they need to get where they want to go. They read some books, follow the markers left by others who have made the trip before, or happily stumble on the right path for them.

Others of us need help: from our friends, our fellow travelers, navigational charts or professional guides. Sometimes, rooting around in the junkyards of our dysfunctional childhood programming, we uncover garbage that has been covered over by our co-dependency. We need to turn to special sources for help to further our progress toward wellness and well-being.

Here are some sources of information to assist you on your journey toward self-realization and self-fulfillment:

Co-dependency

Co-dependents Anonymous
P.O. Box 33577
Phoenix, AZ 85067-3577

There are now about 2,000 Co-dependent Anonymous groups. If you do not find one in the white pages of your telephone book, you can write for information about meeting places or how to start a group.

Depression Or Other Emotional Disorders

Recovery, Inc.
802 N. Dearborn St.
Chicago, IL 60610

This organization will refer you to a supportive group of people who are having difficulty with depression or other emotional problems. Ann Landers says they do a "fabulous" job.

Domestic Violence

Domestic Violence Hotline
Call toll-free 1-(800) 333-SAFE

These people are there for you 24 hours a day, seven days a week. They will refer you to local help.

Life/Career Planning

Career Planning and Adult Development Network
4965 Sierra Road
San Jose, CA 95132

This is a network of professional career counselors and specialists in career development. They can inform you of a member in your area to help you find the career direction that would most contribute to your overall well-being.

Obesity

Obesity Recovery Foundation
P.O. Box 188161
Sacramento, CA 95818

Information about this group came from a woman who once weighed 400 pounds, who is now slim and directs an obesity recovery clinic at a California hospital.

Obsessive-Compulsive Disorders

Obsessive-Compulsive Disorder Foundation
P.O. Box 9573
New Haven, CT 06535

These people provide referrals to treatment centers, coordinate support groups, monitor research and publish a quarterly newsletter.

Obsessive-Compulsive Anonymous
P.O. Box 215
New Hyde Park, NY 11040
(516) 741-4901

Parenting

Parenting Anonymous
6733 S. Sepulveda Blvd.
Los Angeles, CA 90045

Good parenting is not modeled in dysfunctional families. In a PA group you can find support from others who understand the problems of parenting and hear how others solve their parenting problems.

In some areas the YMCA or YWCA offer parenting and family classes and workshops. Many towns have a Parent Center or help for other family problems.

Self-Help

The Self-Help Center
1600 Dodge Ave., Suite S-122
Evanston, IL 60201
(312) 328-0470

It is estimated there are about half a million self-help groups in the United States. They provide referrals and try to keep tabs on new self-help groups as they emerge.

Temperament Type

The Meyers-Briggs Type Indicator is published by Consulting Psychologists Press, 577 College Ave., Palo Alto, CA 94306. It is only available to certain qualified professionals. However, MBTI workshops are offered through many universities and community colleges. You can also get information about the MBTI and workshops by writing the Career Planning and Adult Development Newsletter at the previous address given.

Transactional Analysis Training Or Therapy

International Transactional Analysis Association
1772 Vallejo Street
San Francisco, CA 94123
(415) 885-5992

The I.T.A.A. can refer you to any of over 3,000 accredited TA practitioners or let you know of TA conferences and seminars in your area. Many TA practitioners offer a basic TA 101 training course for beginners. I believe it is an excellent beginning point for anyone who is starting out on the path of self-discovery.

The Well-Being Scale

Gail Sheehy's Well-Being Scale is to be found in her book *Pathfinders*, William Morrow & Company, Inc. NY, 1981. This scale is an excellent device for getting some ideas concerning the well-being of others and how you're doing in your own search for well-being.

Do remember when you seek help from others that your goal is autonomy, not furtherance of your co-dependency. Get all the information and help appropriate to your situation. The final test is how it works for you as you practice autonomy in the world around you.

Que le vaya bien! Which, roughly translated from the Spanish, means, "May all go well with you on your journey."

Notes

Introduction

1. Gerard, D.L., Saenger, G., and Wile, R. The Abstinent Alcoholic, *Archives Of General Psychiatry*, 6:99-111, 1962.

Chapter One

1. Muriel James and Dorothy Jongeward, **Born To Win,** Addison-Wesley. Reading, MA 1971.

2. Christmas Humphreys, **Walk On,** The Theosophical Publishing House, Wheaton, IL 1971 (Quest Book Edition).

3. Eric Berne, **Games People Play,** Grove Press, Inc. New York, NY, 1964.

4. Robert Subby, **Lost In The Shuffle,** Health Communications, Inc., Pompano Beach, FL, 1987.

5. Ruth Fishel, **The Journey Within,** Health Communications, Inc., Pompano Beach, FL, 1987.

Chapter Two

1. Andrew Meacham, "A Travelogue With M. Scott Peck, M.D.," *Changes Magazine*, March/April, 1988.

2. Timmen L. Cermak, M.D., **Diagnosing And Treating Co-dependence,** Johnson Institute Books, Minneapolis, MN, 1986.

3. Eric Berne, M.D., **What Do You Say After You Say Hello?** Grove Press Inc., New York, NY (copyright date not available).

4. Stephen B. Karpman, M.D., "Fairy Tales and Script Drama Analysis," *Transactional Analysis Bulletin*, VII. No. 26, (April, 1986) pp. 39-43.

5. Taibi Kahler, Ph.D. with Hedges Capers, DivM., LHD., "The Miniscript," *Transactional Analysis Journal*, Vol. IV, No. 1, January, 1974.

6. Berne, **What Do You Say After You Say Hello?**

7. Robert L. Goulding, M.D. and Mary McClure Goulding, M.S.W., **The Power Is In The Patient,** TA Press, San Francisco, CA 1978.

8. Robert L. Goulding, M.D., "Foreword," **Success Through Transactional Analysis** by Jut Meininger, Grosset & Dunlap, Publishers, New York, NY, 1973.

9. Charles L. Whitfield, M.D. **Healing The Child Within,** Health Communications, Inc., Pompano Beach, FL, 1987.

10. Sharon Wegscheider-Cruse, "Co-dependency: The Therapeutic Void," *Co-dependency*, Health Communications, Inc., Deerfield Beach, FL, 1989.

11. Eric Berne, M.D., **Principles Of Group Treatment,** Oxford University Press, New York, NY, 1966.

Chapter Three

1. Eric Berne, M.D., **What Do You Say After You Say Hello?,** Grove Press, Inc., New York, NY (copyright date not available).

2. Berne, **What Do You Say After You Say Hello?**

3. Paul McCormack and Leonard Campos, **Introduce Yourself To Transactional Analysis,** San Joaquin TA Study Group, Stockton, CA, 1969.

4. Claude Steiner, **Games Alcoholics Play: The Analysis Of Life Scripts,** Grove Press, Inc., New York, NY, 1971.

5. Muriel James and Dorothy Jongeward, **Born To Win,** Addison-Wesley Publishing Co., Reading MA, 1971.

6. Charles L. Whitfield, M.D., **Healing The Child Within,** Health Communications, Inc., Pompano Beach, FL, 1987.

Chapter Four

1. Eric Berne, M.D., **The Structure And Dynamics Of Groups,** Grove Press, Inc., New York, NY, 1963.

2. Timmen L. Cermak, M.D., **Diagnosing And Treating Co-dependence,** Johnson Institute Books, Minneapolis, MN, 1986.

Chapter Five

1. Janet Woititz, **Adult Children Of Alcoholics,** Health Communications, Inc., Pompano Beach, FL, 1983.

2. William C. Schutz, **Joy,** Irvington Publications, New York, NY, 1967.

3. Charles L. Whitfield, **Healing The Child Within,** Health Communications, Inc., Pompano Beach, FL, 1987.

4. Eric Berne, M.D., **What Do You Say After You Say Hello?,** Grove Press, Inc., New York, NY (copyright date not available).

5. Eric Berne, M.D., **Transactional Analysis In Psychotherapy,** Grove Press Inc., New York, NY, 1961.

7. Eric Berne, M.D., **Games People Play,** Grove Press Inc., New York, NY, 1964.

8. Ronald Shlensky, M.D., J.D., "Anxiety and Fear: A Treatable Disorder," *Sansum Highlights,* Vol. 12, Number 2, Spring, Santa Barbara, CA, 1989.

Chapter Six

1. Robert L. Goulding, M.D. and Mary McClure Goulding, M.S.W., **The Power Is In The Patient,** TA Press, San Francisco, CA, 1978.

2. Richard Cornuelle, **De-Managing America,** Random House, New York, NY, 1975.

3. Eric Berne, M.D., **What Do You Say After You Say Hello?,** Grove Press, Inc., New York, NY (copyright date not available).

4. Mary McClure Goulding, M.S.W. and Robert L. Goulding, M.D., **Changing Lives Through Redecision Therapy,** Brunner/Mazel Publisher, New York, NY, 1979.

Chapter Seven

1. Eric Berne, M.D., **What Do You Say After You Say Hello?,** Grove Press, Inc., New York, NY (copyright date not available).

2. Abraham H. Maslow, **Toward A Psychology Of Being,** Van Nostrand Reinhold Company, New York, NY, 1962.

3. Gail Sheehy, **Pathfinders,** William Morrow & Co., Inc., New York, NY, 1981.

4. Gail Sheehy, **Pathfinders.**

5. John Bradshaw, Unpublished papers, 1986.

6. Everett L. Shostrom, **Man, The Manipulator,** Abingdon Press, Nashville, TN, 1967.

7. Maxwell Maltz, **The Magic Power Of Self Image Psychology,** Prentice Hall, Inc., Englewood Cliffs, NJ

8. Joe Alexander, **Dare To Change,** New American Library, Broadway, NY, 1984.

Chapter Eight

1. David Keirsey and Marlyn Bates, **Please Understand Me,** Prometheus Nemesis Book Company, Del Mar, CA, 1984.

2. Albert Mehrabian "Communications Without Words," *Psychology Today*, 2:53, September, 1968.

3. Carl Rogers, **Some Elements Of Interpersonal Communications,** a talk given at the California Institute of Technology, Pasadena, CA, November 9, 1964.

4. **The Random House Dictionary Of The English Language,** Random House, New York, NY, 1966.

5. Janet Geringer Woititz, **Struggle For Intimacy,** Health Communications, Pompano Beach, FL, 1985.

6. Muriel James and James Savary, **The Heart Of Friendship,** Harper and Row, Publishers, San Francisco, CA, 1978.

Chapter Nine

1. Pia Mellody, **Facing Co-dependency,** Harper & Row, Publishers, San Francisco, CA, 1989.

2. Charles A. Garfield with Hal Zina Bennett, **Peak Performance,** Jeremy P. Tarcher, Los Angeles, CA, 1984.

3. Timmen L. Cermak, **Diagnosing And Treating Co-dependence,** Johnson Institute Books, Minneapolis, MN, 1986.

4. Edmund Jacobsen, **You Must Relax,** McGraw-Hill Book Company, Inc., New York, NY, 1957.

Chapter Ten

1. Virginia Satir, **peoplemaking,** Science and Behavior Books, Inc., Palo Alto, CA, 1972.